Better Homes and Gardens®

make▶ahead
MEALS

150+ Recipes to Enjoy Every Day of the Week

HOUGHTON MIFFLIN HARCOURT
BOSTON · NEW YORK · 2015

Meredith Corporation

Gayle Goodson Butler
Executive Vice President, Editor in Chief
Better Homes and Gardens® Magazine

Better Homes and Gardens® Make-Ahead Meals

Editor: Jan Miller

Project Editor: Tricia Bergman, Waterbury Publications, Inc.

Contributing Editor: Lisa Kingsley, Waterbury Publications, Inc.

Contributing Copy Editor and Proofreader: Terri Fredrickson, Peg Smith

Test Kitchen Director: Lynn Blanchard

Test Kitchen Product Supervisor: Lori Wilson

Test Kitchen Home Economists: Sarah Brekke; Linda Brewer; Carla Christian, R.D.; Juliana Hale; Sammy Mila; Colleen Weeden

Contributing Photographers: Jason Donnelly, Jacob Fox, Andy Lyons

Contributing Stylists: Greg Luna, Sue Mitchell, Jennifer Peterson, Charlie Worthington

Administrative Assistants: Barb Allen, Marlene Todd

Special Interest Media

Editorial Leader: Doug Kouma

Editorial Director, Food: Jennifer Dorland Darling

Art Director: Gene Rauch

Houghton Mifflin Harcourt

Publisher: Natalie Chapman

Editorial Director: Cindy Kitchel

Executive Editor, Brands: Anne Ficklen

Editorial Associate: Molly Aronica

Managing Editor: Marina Padakis Lowry

Production Director: Tom Hyland

Design Director: Ken Carlson, Waterbury Publications, Inc.

Associate Design Director: Doug Samuelson, Waterbury Publications, Inc.

Production Assistant: Mindy Samuelson, Waterbury Publications, Inc.

www.hmhco.com

Library of Congress Cataloging-in-Publication Data is available

ISBN 978-0-544-45616-7 (pbk)

ISBN 978-0-544-45684-6 (ebk)

Book design by Waterbury Publications, Inc., Des Moines, Iowa.

DOW 10 9 8 7 6 5 4 3 2 1
4500541195
Printed in the United State of America

Our seal assures you that every recipe in *Better Homes and Gardens® Make-Ahead Meals* has been tested in the Better Homes and Gardens® Test Kitchen. This means that each recipe is practical and reliable and meets our high standards of taste appeal. We guarantee your satisfaction with this book for as long as you own it.

contents ▶

saving time ▶

When it comes to mealtimes, there are a couple of things that can be agreed upon: 1. Life is busy. 2. We want to feed our families delicious, nutritious food on a reasonable budget. With a bit of planning, you can make great meals every day of the week. The following strategies in *Better Homes Gardens Make-Ahead Meals* help make it possible.

One Recipe, Many Ways An easy approach to big-batch cooking. Base recipes are made, portioned, and frozen to be used in multiple recipes.

From the Freezer Soups, stews, casseroles, calzones, and entrées go from freezer to oven or stovetop for a hot and hearty meal in short order.

Slow Cooker Recipes Food is prepped the night before and stored in a sealed slow cooker bag in the refrigerator. The next morning, the bag dropped into a slow cooker, and the cooker is set according to recipe directions.

Jump-Start Recipes Recipes are assembled nearly to the point of cooking, then refrigerated until ready to heat and eat—as well as salads and noodle bowls that just need a tossing before serving.

Icons Legend

Recipes are identified with the following icons to help you tailor your meals to your family's needs.

LOW-CAL 400 calories or less per serving for entrées
LOW-CAL 200 calories or less per serving for sweets
MEATLESS No animal products
FEEDS A CROWD 8 servings or more
QUICK Prep time of 30 minutes or fewer

Arrows Legend

Recipes are identified with an arrow icon that tells how far ahead a recipe can be made—from up to 1 day to months ahead.
▸ Make ahead up to 24 hours
▸▸ Make ahead 1 to 3 days
▸▸▸ Make ahead weeks or months

General Make-Ahead Strategies

1. Read The Recipe Even if a recipe isn't specifically make ahead, read through it carefully for steps that can be done ahead without compromising flavor, texture, or appearance. With the exception of fruits and vegetables that oxidize and turn brown when exposed to air—such as potatoes, apples, pears, root vegetables, bananas and avocados—most peeling, seeding, and chopping can be done ahead of time. Prepped produce can be stored in the refrigerator, tightly covered, up to 1 day. Vegetables such as green beans and Brussels sprouts can be blanched and stored in the refrigerator.

2. Use Time Wisely Have a few spare minutes? Use even a small window of time to make a grocery list or a weekly meal plan. Cut up vegetables, sauté mushrooms, or caramelize and refrigerate onions. Roast a whole chicken or a pork loin roast and store it to use in main-dish salads or casseroles.

3. Be Efficient When prepping for a recipe that calls for all the produce to be added at the same time, reduce the use of containers, consolidate prep and cooking steps, and cut cleanup by layering and storing all the produce in one container.

4. Prep Smart Know what you can and can't prep or cook ahead. Most vegetables that are going to be cooked can be chopped ahead of time, but if they are going to be served raw, they should be prepared as close to serving time as possible. Fresh herbs should be chopped right before using because cutting causes them to wilt and break down. Most salads can be made ahead and refrigerated—if the vegetables and greens are kept separate from the dressing. Dress the salad right before serving. Both pasta and rice can be cooked al dente, then cooled and stored in the refrigerator for a day or two. When they are reheated in a microwave with just a little water, they maintain most of the textural quality.

5. Create a Repertoire Hearty braises, soups, and stews improve with a little age. Grilled and pan-seared foods are best served right after cooking. Even when the main part of a recipe can't be made ahead, often the most time-consuming steps—sauces, seasoning pastes, chutneys, relishes, dressings, and flavored butters—can be. Pie pastry, pizza dough, and cookie dough can all be made ahead and chilled or frozen.

tools

For any make-ahead strategy—prepping and storing, making a base recipe for multiple dishes, freezing, or slow cooking—having the right equipment for preparation, storage, and cooking will ease the job while ensuring that the dishes you sit down to enjoy are high quality. While there is crossover among strategies in terms of the equipment you use, the items shown and listed on these pages will serve you well.

jump-start recipes
- Mixing and prep bowls in a variety of sizes
- Tightly sealed plastic or glass containers in a variety of sizes
- Quality plastic wrap that seals tightly
- Aluminum foil
- 13×9×2-inch baking dish(es)

one recipe, many ways
- Large rimmed baking sheets (15×10×1)
- Large skillet(s)
- Large saucepan(s)
- 4-quart Dutch oven
- 5- to 6-quart Dutch oven
- 8-quart Dutch oven

from the freezer
- Sturdy, tightly sealed plastic or glass containers in a variety of sizes
- Freezer-quality plastic wrap
- Freezer-quality aluminum foil
- Resealable plastic bags in 1-quart, gallon, and 2-gallon sizes (see tip on page 135)
- Masking tape or labels for dating and labeling food
- Permanent marker for dating and labeling food

slow cooker recipes
- 3½- or 4-quart slow cooker
- 5- to 7-quart slow cooker
- Slow-cooker liners

sweets to share
- Aluminum baking pans in an array of sizes (9- or 10-inch pie pans, loaf pans, 8-inch square, 13×9×2-inch). Plus covered pans to tote desserts to gatherings.
- Waxed paper to layer cookies, brownies, and bars in freezer containers

one recipe
MANY WAYS

Make a base recipe—from meat, vegetables, grains, or legumes, plus seasonings—then chill or freeze them in portions. Add portions to a few more recipe ingredients for flavorful quick-to-the-table dishes.

recipes

▸ HOURS AHEAD   ▸▸ DAY OR DAYS AHEAD   ▸▸▸ WEEKS OR MONTHS AHEAD

▶▶▶ breakfast meat base

MAKE AHEAD UP TO 3 MONTHS

PREP: 10 minutes   COOK: 25 minutes   MAKES: 9 1-cup portions

- 8 ounces bacon, coarsely chopped
- 2 pounds bulk pork sausage
- 1½ cups chopped onion (3 medium)
- 4 cloves garlic, minced
- 1 16-ounce package diced ham
- ¼ cup snipped fresh Italian (flat-leaf) parsley
- ½ teaspoon black pepper

1. In a large skillet cook bacon over medium heat until crisp. Remove bacon with a slotted spoon and drain on paper towels. Drain bacon fat from skillet; discard. Return skillet to medium-high heat. Add sausage, onion, and garlic. Cook until meat is brown, using a wooden spoon to break up meat as it cooks. Drain off fat. Stir in reserved bacon, ham, parsley, and pepper. Cool.

2. To store, place breakfast meat base in 1-cup portions in airtight containers or freezer containers. Cover and store in the refrigerator up to 3 days or freeze up to 3 months. If frozen, thaw in the refrigerator overnight before using.

base recipe ▶

savory breakfast muffins

PREP: 30 minutes   BAKE: 15 minutes at 400°F   COOL: 5 minutes   MAKES: 12 servings

Nonstick cooking spray
1 cup all-purpose flour
½ cup yellow cornmeal
2 tablespoons sugar
2½ teaspoons baking powder
1 cup milk
¼ cup vegetable oil or butter, melted
2 eggs
1 portion Breakfast Meat Base (1 cup), thawed (see recipe, page 13)
½ cup shredded cheddar cheese
Maple syrup (optional)

1. Preheat oven to 400°F. Lightly coat six 3¼-inch (jumbo) muffin cups (see tip below for smaller muffin cups) with nonstick cooking spray; set aside. In a medium bowl stir together flour, cornmeal, sugar, and baking powder. In a small bowl combine milk, oil, and eggs. Add milk mixture to flour mixture all at once and whisk until combined. Fold in Breakfast Meat Base and cheese. Spoon batter into prepared muffin cups.

2. Bake for 15 to 17 minutes or until light brown and a wooden toothpick inserted near centers comes out clean. Cool in muffin cups on a wire rack for 5 minutes. Run a small metal spatula or knife around edges of muffins; remove from pans. If desired, serve warm with maple syrup.

Per serving: *182 cal., 10 g fat (3 g sat. fat), 46 mg chol., 254 mg sodium, 16 g carb., 1 g fiber, 7 g pro.*

If you do not have a jumbo muffin pan, divide the muffin batter among twelve 2½-inch muffin cups and bake for 12 to 14 minutes.

sunrise omelet

PREP: 20 minutes   COOK: 20 minutes   MAKES: 4 servings

  3 **tablespoons butter**
½ **cup chopped green sweet pepper**
¼ **cup chopped onion**
½ **cup chopped roma tomatoes**
  1 **portion Breakfast Meat Base (1 cup), thawed (see recipe, page 13)**
  8 **eggs**
¼ **teaspoon black pepper**
⅔ **cup shredded cheddar cheese**
   Chopped roma tomatoes (optional)
   Shredded cheddar cheese (optional)

1. For filling, in a 10-inch nonstick skillet with flared sides melt 1 tablespoon of the butter over medium heat. Add sweet pepper and onion. Cook and stir about 5 minutes or until vegetables are tender. Add the ½ cup tomatoes and Breakfast Meat Base. Cook and stir for 2 minutes more or until heated through. Remove from skillet; set aside. Wipe skillet clean.

2. In a medium bowl whisk together eggs and black pepper until combined but not frothy; set aside.

3. In the same skillet melt ½ tablespoon of the remaining butter over medium heat. Pour in one-fourth of the egg mixture (about ½ cup). As eggs set, run a spatula around the edge of the skillet, lifting eggs so uncooked portion flows underneath. When eggs are set but still shiny, spoon one-fourth of the Breakfast Meat Base across the center of the omelet. Sprinkle with one-fourth of the cheese.

4. Fold one edge of the omelet about a third of the way toward the center. Fold the opposite edge toward the center. Transfer omelet onto a plate. Repeat with the remaining butter, egg mixture, Breakfast Meat Base, and cheese to make four omelets. If desired, sprinkle with additional chopped tomatoes and cheese.

Per serving: *406 cal., 31 g fat (15 g sat. fat), 441 mg chol., 640 mg sodium, 5 g carb., 1 g fiber, 25 g pro.*

breakfast burritos

START TO FINISH: 30 minutes   MAKES: 4 servings

     2 **tablespoons butter**
     1 **cup refrigerated shredded hash brown potatoes**
     1 **clove garlic, minced**
   ¼ **teaspoon ground cumin**
     3 **eggs**
     2 **tablespoons milk**
   ⅛ **teaspoon black pepper**
     1 **portion Breakfast Meat Base (1 cup), thawed (see recipe, page 13)**
     1 **4½-ounce can diced green chile peppers, drained**
     4 **10-inch flour tortillas**
   ⅔ **cup shredded Monterey Jack cheese or cheddar cheese**
        Red and/or green salsa

1. For the potatoes, in a large nonstick skillet heat 1 tablespoon of the butter over medium heat until melted. Stir in potatoes, garlic, and cumin. Spread in an even layer; press down lightly with a spatula. Cook for 6 to 7 minutes or until golden brown on the bottom. Turn potatoes over; spread evenly and press down lightly. Cook for 6 to 8 minutes more or until golden brown and crisp. Remove from skillet; set aside. Keep warm.

2. For the scrambled eggs and meat, in a small bowl whisk together eggs, milk, and pepper. In the same skillet heat the remaining 1 tablespoon butter over medium heat until melted. Pour in egg mixture. Cook, without stirring, until eggs begin to set on the bottom and around edges. Using a spatula or large spoon, lift and fold the partially cooked egg so the uncooked portion flows underneath. Stir in Breakfast Meat Base and chile peppers; continue cooking for 2 to 3 minutes more or until eggs are cooked through but still glossy and moist. Remove from heat.

3. Stack tortillas and wrap in microwave-safe paper towels. Microwave on 100 percent power (high) for 30 seconds or until heated through. Divide potatoes among tortillas, placing just below the center of each tortilla. Top with scrambled eggs and cheese. Fold bottom edge up and over the filling. Fold opposite sides in. Roll up from bottom. Serve with salsa.

Per serving: *535 cal., 27 g fat (13 g sat. fat), 198 mg chol., 1,201 mg sodium, 49 g carb., 4 g fiber, 24 g pro.*

▶▶ meat-lover's breakfast casserole

MAKE AHEAD UP TO 2 DAYS

PREP: 25 minutes   BAKE: 45 minutes at 350°F   STAND: 10 minutes   MAKES: 6 servings

Nonstick cooking spray
3 cups frozen shredded hash brown potatoes
2 portions Breakfast Meat Base (2 cups), thawed (see recipe, page 13)
¾ cup shredded Monterey Jack cheese with jalapeño peppers or cheddar cheese (3 ounces)

¼ cup sliced green onions (2)
4 eggs, lightly beaten, or 1 cup refrigerated or frozen egg product, thawed
1½ cups milk
⅛ teaspoon salt
⅛ teaspoon black pepper

1. Preheat oven to 350°F. Coat a 2-quart square baking dish with cooking spray. Spread potatoes evenly in the bottom of the prepared baking dish. Sprinkle with Breakfast Meat Base, cheese, and green onions.

2. In a medium bowl combine eggs, milk, salt, and pepper. Pour egg mixture over potato mixture in dish.*

3. Bake, uncovered, for 45 minutes or until a knife inserted near the center comes out clean. Let stand for 10 minutes before serving.

Per serving: *293 cal., 18 g fat (8 g sat. fat), 176 mg chol., 612 mg sodium, 12 g carb., 1 g fiber, 20 g pro.*

MEAT-LOVER'S BREAKFAST CASSEROLE FOR 12: Prepare as directed, except double all of the ingredients and use a 3-quart rectangular baking dish. Bake, uncovered, for 55 to 60 minutes or until a knife inserted near the center comes out clean. Let stand for 10 minutes before serving.

*To make and store casserole until ready to serve, prepare as directed through Step 2. Cover and chill for 2 to 24 hours. To serve, preheat oven to 350°F. Bake, uncovered, for 50 to 55 minutes or until a knife inserted near the center comes out clean. Let stand for 10 minutes before serving.

italian frittata

START TO FINISH: 25 minutes   MAKES: 4 servings

8	eggs, lightly beaten
¼	cup grated Parmesan cheese
1	tablespoon snipped fresh basil
¼	teaspoon crushed red pepper
¼	teaspoon salt
¼	teaspoon black pepper
3	cloves garlic, minced
1	tablespoon olive oil
1	cup chopped zucchini
1	portion Breakfast Meat Base (1 cup), thawed (see recipe, page 13)
2	roma tomatoes, sliced
1	cup shredded mozzarella cheese (4 ounces)
	Snipped fresh basil (optional)

1. In a medium bowl combine eggs, 2 tablespoons of the Parmesan cheese, the 1 tablespoon basil, crushed red pepper, salt, and pepper; set aside. In a large broiler-proof skillet cook garlic in hot oil over medium heat for 30 seconds. Add zucchini; cook and stir about 5 minutes or until crisp-tender. Stir in Breakfast Meat Base.

2. Set oven top rack 4 to 5 inches from broiler. Preheat broiler. Pour egg mixture over meat mixture in skillet. Cook over medium heat. As mixture sets, run a spatula around edge of skillet, lifting egg mixture so uncooked portion flows underneath. Continue cooking and lifting edges until egg mixture is almost set (surface will be moist). Arrange tomato slices on top of egg mixture. Sprinkle with remaining Parmesan cheese and the mozzarella cheese.

3. Place skillet under the broiler 4 to 5 inches from heat. Broil for 2 to 3 minutes or just until top is set and cheese is melted. (Or bake in a preheated 400°F oven for 5 minutes until top is set.) Let stand for 5 minutes before serving. Cut into wedges and garnish with basil, if desired.

Per serving: *383 cal., 26 g fat (10 g sat. fat), 420 mg chol., 845 mg sodium, 7 g carb., 1 g fiber, 29 g pro.*

▶▶▶ ground beef base

MAKE AHEAD UP TO 3 MONTHS

START TO FINISH: 35 minutes   MAKES: 11 1-cup portions

        4 pounds ground beef
    1½ cups chopped onions (3 medium)
        1 cup chopped carrots (2 medium)
      ½ cup chopped celery (1 stalk)
        4 cloves garlic, minced
        1 teaspoon salt
      ½ teaspoon black pepper

1. In a 5- to 6-quart Dutch oven cook ground beef, onions, carrots, celery, and garlic over medium-high heat until meat is browned, using a wooden spoon to break up meat as it cooks. Drain off fat. Stir in salt and pepper.

2. To store, place Ground Beef Base in freezer containers. Cover and store in the refrigerator up to 3 days or freeze for up to 3 months. If frozen, thaw portions in the refrigerator overnight.

base recipes ▶

▶▶▶ tomato base

MAKE AHEAD UP TO 3 MONTHS

PREP: 20 minutes   COOK: 30 minutes   MAKES: 6 1-cup portions

- 2 tablespoons olive oil
- 5 cloves garlic, smashed
- ¼ teaspoon crushed red pepper
- 2 28-ounce cans diced tomatoes, undrained
- ½ cup dry red wine
- ⅓ cup tomato paste
- 2 teaspoons packed brown sugar
- 1 teaspoon salt

1. In a large saucepan heat oil over medium heat. Add garlic and crushed red pepper; cook and stir for 3 to 4 minutes or until garlic is golden. Carefully stir in tomatoes, wine, tomato paste, brown sugar, and salt.

2. Bring to boiling; reduce heat. Simmer, uncovered, for 30 to 40 minutes or until slightly thickened and reduced by about one-third, stirring occasionally (you should have about 6 cups).

3. To store, place Tomato Base in 1-cup portions in airtight storage containers or freezer containers. Cover and store in the refrigerator up to 3 days or freeze up to 3 months. If frozen, thaw portions in the refrigerator overnight.

cheeseburger pizza

PREP: 45 minutes   BAKE: 12 minutes at 425°F   MAKES: 8 servings

Vegetable oil
Cornmeal
1 recipe Pizza Dough, thawed if frozen
2 portions Ground Beef Base (2 cups), thawed (see recipe, page 24)
4 slices bacon, crisply cooked and crumbled (optional)
1 portion Tomato Base (1 cup), thawed (see recipe, page 25)
2 tablespoons yellow mustard
1 tablespoon packed brown sugar
1 tablespoon cider vinegar
1 8-ounce package shredded triple-cheddar blend with cream cheese
½ cup dill pickle slices
1 cup shredded lettuce

1. Preheat oven to 425°F. Grease an extra-large baking sheet with vegetable oil; sprinkle with cornmeal. Set aside. Roll each portion of Pizza Dough into an 11-inch circle. Prick evenly with the tines of a fork. Place dough circles on the prepared baking sheet. Bake for 5 minutes or until crusts are set but not brown. Transfer to wire racks.

2. Meanwhile, for toppings, in a medium bowl combine 1½ cups of the Ground Beef Base and, if desired, crumbled bacon. (Use remaining ½ cup Ground Beef Base in another recipe.) Add Tomato Base, mustard, brown sugar, and vinegar.

3. Place each pizza on a baking sheet. Evenly divide toppings between pizza crusts then sprinkle with cheese. Bake for 12 to 14 minutes or until crust is golden and cheese is melted. Top with pickles and lettuce.

PIZZA DOUGH: In a large mixing bowl combine 1¼ cups flour, 1 package active yeast, and ½ teaspoon salt; add 1 cup warm water (120°F to 130°F) and 2 tablespoons olive oil. Beat with an electric mixer on low speed for 30 seconds, scraping sides of the bowl. Beat on high speed 3 minutes. Using a wooden spoon, stir in as much 1¼ to 1¾ cups flour as you can. Turn dough out onto a lightly floured surface. Knead in enough of the flour to make a moderately stiff dough that is smooth and elastic (6 to 8 minutes total). Divide dough in half. Cover; let rest for 10 minutes. If desired, wrap each portion in plastic wrap and place in airtight containers. Chill up to 24 hours or freeze up to 3 months. Thaw dough in the refrigerator. Let stand at room temperature for 30 minutes.

Per serving: *400 cal., 20 g fat (9 g sat. fat), 54 mg chol., 701 mg sodium, 39 g carb., 3 g fiber, 18 g pro.*

TIP

Convenience products such as cooked bacon, shredded cheese, and frozen hash browns are partially prepared as purchased. Call on these and others to cut prep and cleanup time.

beef samosas

PREP: 30 minutes   BAKE: 25 minutes at 400°F   MAKES: 6 servings

 1 recipe Pastry Dough, thawed if frozen
 2 portions Ground Beef Base (2 cups), thawed (see recipe, page 24)
 1 cup frozen shredded hash brown potatoes
 ½ cup frozen peas
 2 teaspoons grated fresh ginger
1½ teaspoons garam masala
 1 fresh serrano chile pepper, seeded and finely chopped (see tip, below)
 1 egg, lightly beaten
 1 tablespoon water
   Mango chutney

1. Preheat oven to 400°F. Divide Pastry Dough into thirds. On a lightly floured surface, roll each portion into a 10-inch circle. Cut each circle in half.

2. For filling, in a large bowl combine Ground Beef Base, hash brown potatoes, peas, ginger, garam masala, and serrano pepper. Spoon filling onto pastry half-circles. In a small bowl combine egg and the water. Brush edges of pastry with some of the egg mixture. Fold pastry in half over filling; seal with the tines of a fork. Prick tops of samosas with fork; brush with the remaining egg mixture. Place samosas on a baking sheet.

3. Bake for 25 to 30 minutes or until heated through and pastry is golden. Serve with mango chutney.

PASTRY DOUGH: In a large bowl stir together 2½ cups all-purpose flour and 1 teaspoon salt. Using a pastry blender, cut in ½ cup shortening and ¼ cup cut-up butter, until pieces are peasize. Sprinkle 1 tablespoon ice water over part of the flour mixture; toss with a fork. Push moistened dough to the side of the bowl. Repeat moistening flour mixture, 1 tablespoon ice water at a time, until all is moistened. Gather dough into a ball, kneading gently until it holds together.

Per serving: *699 cal., 35 g fat (13 g sat. fat), 94 mg chol., 955 mg sodium, 74 g carb., 2 g fiber, 20 g pro.*

Chile peppers contain oils that can burn your skin and eyes. These oils are released when the chiles are cut. When working with chiles, wear plastic or rubber gloves. If your bare hands do touch the cut peppers, wash your hands and nails well with soap and warm water.

beef enchiladas

PREP: 35 minutes   BAKE: 35 minutes at 350°F   MAKES: 8 servings

  1 **recipe Enchilada Sauce**
 ¾ **cup chicken broth**
 ⅓ **cup uncooked long grain rice**
  1 **teaspoon finely chopped canned chipotle peppers in adobo sauce (see tip, page 29)**
 ¼ **teaspoon salt**
  1 **portion Tomato Base (1 cup), thawed (see recipe, page 25)**
  2 **portions Ground Beef Base (2 cups), thawed (see recipe, page 24)**
  1 **15-ounce can pinto beans, rinsed and drained**
     Nonstick cooking spray
  8 **8-inch flour tortillas**
1½ **cups shredded Monterey Jack cheese (6 ounces)**
     Quartered cherry tomatoes (optional)
     Snipped fresh cilantro (optional)

1. Preheat oven to 350°F. Prepare Enchilada Sauce; set aside. In a small saucepan bring broth to boiling. Stir in rice, chipotle pepper, and salt. Reduce heat. Simmer, covered, about 15 minutes or until rice is tender and broth is absorbed. Stir in ½ cup of the Tomato Base. (Use remaining ½ cup Tomato Base in another recipe.) Spread rice in a shallow baking pan to cool for 10 minutes.

2. For the filling, in a large bowl combine Ground Beef Base, beans, and the cooled rice.

3. Coat a 3-quart rectangular baking dish with cooking spray. Spread about ¾ cup Enchilada Sauce in the baking dish. To assemble enchiladas, place about ½ cup of the filling on each tortilla. Roll tortilla around filling. Arrange in baking dish, seams side up. Spoon remaining Enchilada Sauce over tortillas.

4. Bake for 25 minutes. Sprinkle with cheese. Bake about 10 minutes more or until heated through. If desired, top with cherry tomatoes and cilantro.

ENCHILADA SAUCE: In a medium saucepan combine one 14.5-ounce can diced fire-roasted tomatoes with garlic, undrained; ½ cup salsa; 1½ teaspoons ground ancho pepper; and 1 teaspoon unsweetened cocoa powder. Bring to boiling; reduce heat. Simmer, uncovered, for 10 minutes or until slightly thickened, stirring occasionally. Cool slightly. Transfer to a food processor or blender. Cover and process or blend until nearly smooth.

Per serving: *421 cal., 17 g fat (7 g sat. fat), 51 mg chol., 1,186 mg sodium, 45 g carb., 2 g fiber, 22 g pro.*

The Enchilada Sauce for these beefy enchiladas can be prepared ahead. Cool, then store in a tightly covered container in the refrigerator up to 2 days or freeze up to 1 month.

▶▶▶ rolled lasagna florentine

MAKE AHEAD UP TO 2 MONTHS

PREP: 35 minutes   BAKE: 1 hour 15 minutes at 350°F   MAKES: 6 servings

- 1 egg, lightly beaten
- 1 15-ounce carton ricotta cheese
- ¼ teaspoon salt
- ¼ teaspoon black pepper
- 1 8-ounce package shredded Italian cheese blend (2 cups)
- 1 10-ounce package frozen chopped spinach, thawed and squeezed dry
- 12 dried lasagna noodles, cooked according to package directions
- 2 portions Tomato Base (2 cups), thawed (see recipe, page 25)
- 1 portion Ground Beef Base (1 cup), thawed (see recipe, page 24)
- 1½ teaspoons dried Italian seasoning, crushed
- ¼ teaspoon fennel seeds, crushed

1. Preheat oven to 350°F. For spinach filling, in a medium bowl combine egg, ricotta cheese, salt, and pepper. Stir in 1 cup of the Italian cheese blend and the spinach. Spread filling on cooked lasagna noodles. Starting from a narrow end, roll up each noodle.

2. For meat sauce, in a medium bowl combine Tomato Base, Ground Beef Base, Italian seasoning, and fennel seeds.

3. Spread ½ cup of the meat sauce in a 2-quart rectangular baking dish. Arrange lasagna rolls on sauce in baking dish. Top with the remaining meat sauce and sprinkle with the remaining 1 cup Italian cheese blend.*

4. Cover with greased or nonstick foil. Bake for 1¼ to 1½ hours or until heated through.

Per serving: 562 cal., 26 g fat (14 g sat. fat), 115 mg chol., 970 mg sodium, 48 g carb., 5 g fiber, 33 g pro.

*To make and freeze casserole, cover baking dish with plastic wrap. Place casserole in a resealable freezer bag. Seal and freeze up to 2 months. To serve, thaw in the refrigerator overnight. Preheat oven to 350°F. Remove plastic wrap; cover with greased or nonstick foil. Bake for 1¼ to 1½ hours or until heated through.

pastitsio

PREP: 30 minutes   BAKE: 45 minutes at 350°F   STAND: 10 minutes   MAKES: 8 servings

  6 ounces dried cavatappi or penne pasta
  2 portions Ground Beef Base (2 cups), thawed (see recipe, page 24)
  2 portions Tomato Base (2 cups), thawed (see recipe, page 25)
  ½ teaspoon ground cinnamon
  ¼ teaspoon ground nutmeg
  ¼ teaspoon fennel seeds, crushed
1½ cups shredded Kasseri cheese or Parmesan cheese (6 ounces)
  1 egg, lightly beaten
  1 15- to 16-ounce jar Alfredo pasta sauce

1. Cook pasta according to package directions; drain. Rinse with cold water until cool; drain again. In a large bowl combine cooked pasta, Ground Beef Base, 1½ cups of the Tomato Base, cinnamon, nutmeg, and fennel seeds. Stir in ½ cup of the cheese. Divide mixture among eight 8-ounce ramekins or individual casseroles, or spread in one 2-quart square baking dish.

2. Preheat oven to 350°F. In a medium bowl combine egg, Alfredo sauce, and the remaining 1 cup cheese. Spread sauce mixture over pasta mixture.

3. If using ramekins, place on a baking sheet. Bake pastitsio in ramekins for 45 minutes; bake pastitio in baking dish about 1¼ hours, or until heated through. Let stand for 10 to 15 minutes before serving.

Per serving: *388 cal., 23 g fat (12 g sat. fat), 122 mg chol., 922 mg sodium, 24 g carb., 2 g fiber, 19 g pro.*

▶▶▶ shredded pork base

MAKE AHEAD UP TO 3 MONTHS

PREP: 25 minutes   BAKE: 3 hours at 325°F   MAKES: 10 1-cup portions

- 2 3- to 3½-pound boneless pork shoulder roasts
- 12 cloves garlic, minced, or 2 tablespoons bottled minced garlic
- 1 tablespoon ground coriander
- 1 tablespoon ground cumin
- 1 tablespoon dried oregano, crushed
- 2 teaspoons onion powder
- 1 teaspoon salt
- 1 teaspoon cayenne pepper
- ½ teaspoon black pepper
- 2 to 3 tablespoons vegetable oil
- 1 14.5-ounce can beef broth

1. Preheat oven to 325°F. Trim fat from meat. For spice rub, in a small bowl combine garlic, coriander, cumin, oregano, onion powder, salt, cayenne pepper, and black pepper. Sprinkle spice mixture evenly over meat; rub in with your fingers.

2. In an 8-quart Dutch oven cook meat in hot oil over medium-high heat until browned on all sides. Pour broth over meat. Bring to boiling; cover Dutch oven. Transfer Dutch oven to the preheated oven. Bake for 3 to 3½ hours or until meat is very tender.

3. Using a slotted spatula or spoon, remove meat from Dutch oven, reserving cooking liquid. Using two forks, pull meat apart into shreds. Skim fat from cooking liquid. Stir enough of the cooking liquid into shredded meat to moisten.

4. To store, place shredded pork in 1-cup portions in airtight containers or freezer containers. Cover and store in the refrigerator up to 3 days or freeze up to 3 months. If frozen, thaw portions in the refrigerator overnight.

base recipe▶

caribbean pork nachos

PREP: 15 minutes   BAKE: 10 minutes at 350°F   MAKES: 6 servings

1 10-ounce package large tortilla chips
1 tablespoon olive oil
1 medium onion, cut into thin wedges
2 teaspoons grated fresh ginger
½ teaspoon ground allspice
2 portions Shredded Pork Base
   (2 cups), thawed (see page 35)
1 15-ounce can black beans, rinsed and
   drained

1 cup purchased salsa
2 tablespoons lime juice
1½ cups shredded Mexican-style four
   cheese blend (6 ounces)
¼ cup sliced green onions (2)
   Snipped fresh cilantro (optional)
¾ cup sour cream
   Salsa (optional)

1. Preheat oven to 350°F. Spread half the tortilla chips on a 12-inch ovenproof platter or pizza pan; set aside.

2. In a large nonstick skillet heat oil over medium heat. Add onion, fresh ginger, and allspice. Cook and stir until onion is tender. Add Shredded Pork Base; heat through. Set aside.

3. In a small bowl stir together black beans, salsa, and lime juice. Set aside.

4. Top chips with half the pork mixture and half the salsa bean mixture. Top with remaining chips, pork, and salsa bean mixture. Sprinkle chips with cheese. Bake for 10 minutes or until cheese is melted.

5. Top with green onions and cilantro, if desired. Serve with sour cream and, if desired, salsa.

Per serving: *604 cal., 32 g fat (11 g sat. fat), 93 mg chol., 1,125 mg sodium, 50 g carb., 7 g fiber, 33 g pro.*

pork and hummus wraps

START TO FINISH: 20 minutes   MAKES: 4 servings

1 7-ounce container roasted garlic hummus (about ¾ cup)
¼ cup chopped fresh cilantro
3 tablespoons lime juice
1 teaspoon chili powder
¼ teaspoon crushed red pepper
1 tablespoon olive oil

2 portions Shredded Pork Base (2 cups), thawed (see recipe, page 35)
½ teaspoon dried oregano, crushed
¼ teaspoon salt
4 8-inch flour tortillas
2 cups shredded fresh spinach
1 small red sweet pepper, cut into strips (⅔ cup)

1. In a small bowl stir together hummus, cilantro, 1 tablespoon of the lime juice, ½ teaspoon of the chili powder, and the crushed red pepper. Set aside.

2. In a large nonstick skillet heat oil over medium heat. Add Shredded Pork Base, remaining ½ teaspoon chili powder, the oregano, and salt. Cook and stir for 2 to 3 minutes or until pork is heated through. Remove from heat and stir in the remaining 2 tablespoons lime juice.

3. To assemble wraps, evenly spread hummus mixture on tortillas. Top with spinach, sweet pepper strips, and pork. Roll up.

Per serving: *516 cal., 26 g fat (5 g sat. fat), 81 mg chol., 1,127 mg sodium, 36 g carb., 4 g fiber, 35 g pro.*

Wraps are the ultimate portable lunch. If you tote them, fold in both ends like a burrito to hold the filling in place.

spicy pork pot stickers with ginger dipping sauce

PREP: 30 minutes   COOK: 5 minutes   MAKES: 4 servings

      1 portion Shredded Pork Base (1 cup), thawed and chopped (see page 35)
   ¼ cup finely chopped onion
      2 tablespoons snipped fresh cilantro
      1 tablespoon reduced-sodium soy sauce
      1 teaspoon grated fresh ginger
      1 clove garlic, minced
   ¼ teaspoon crushed red pepper
      1 egg white
      1 tablespoon water
    20 wonton wrappers
      1 tablespoon canola oil
   ½ cup water
      1 recipe Ginger Dipping Sauce

1. Lightly flour a baking sheet; set aside. For filling, in a large bowl combine Shredded Pork Base, onion, cilantro, soy sauce, ginger, garlic, and crushed red pepper.

2. In a small bowl lightly beat together egg white and the 1 tablespoon water. For pot stickers, spoon about 1 tablespoon of the filling into the center of each wonton wrapper. Brush edges with egg white mixture. Fold wrappers in half across filling, bringing opposite diagonal corners together. Pleat edges then press to seal. Arrange each pot sticker on prepared baking sheet; cover with a clean damp kitchen towel while filling remaining wrappers.

3. In an extra-large nonstick skillet heat oil over medium-high heat. Arrange pot stickers in the skillet so they don't touch. Cook for 2 to 3 minutes or until lightly browned on the bottom. Carefully add the ½ cup water to the skillet. Cover; reduce heat. Cook for 3 to 5 minutes more or until golden brown.

4. Meanwhile, stir together Ginger Dipping Sauce to serve with pot stickers.

GINGER DIPPING SAUCE: In a small bowl combine ¼ cup reduced-sodium soy sauce, ¼ cup rice vinegar, 3 tablespoons chopped green onions, 2 teaspoons grated fresh ginger, ½ teaspoon sugar, and ¼ teaspoon toasted sesame oil.

Per serving: *287 cal., 9 g fat (2 g sat. fat), 44 mg chol., 1,072 mg sodium, 29 g carb., 1 g fiber, 19 g pro.*

Make the Ginger Dipping Sauce minus the green onions several hours ahead to store, covered, in the refrigerator until serving time. Add the green onions right before serving to keep them crisp and fresh.

▶▶ fiesta pork and corn salad

MAKE AHEAD UP TO 2 DAYS

START TO FINISH: 30 minutes   MAKES: 6 servings

3½ **cups fresh or frozen whole kernel corn**
  1 **cup frozen sweet soybeans (edamame)**
  2 **portions Shredded Pork Base (2 cups), thawed (see recipe, page 35)**
½ **cup chopped red onion**
¼ **cup snipped fresh cilantro**
  1 **fresh jalapeño chile pepper, seeded and finely chopped (see tip, page 29)**
  2 **tablespoons olive oil**
  2 **tablespoons lime juice**
  1 **teaspoon finely shredded lime peel**
½ **teaspoon ground cumin**
½ **teaspoon salt**
  2 **cups cherry or grape tomatoes, halved**

1. In a large saucepan cook corn and soybeans, covered, in enough boiling water to cover for 5 minutes or according to package directions; drain. Rinse with cold water to cool and stop cooking; drain again.

2. In a large bowl stir together corn, soybeans, Shredded Pork Roast, red onion, cilantro, and jalapeño pepper.

3. In a screw-top jar combine olive oil, lime peel, lime juice, cumin, and salt. Cover and shake well.

4. Pour dressing over corn mixture, tossing gently to coat. Gently stir in tomatoes.

Per serving: *298 cal., 13 g fat (3 g sat. fat), 54 mg chol., 398 mg sodium, 25 g carb., 4 g fiber, 24 g pro.*

TIP

To make salad ahead, cover and chill up to 24 hours. Let stand for 30 minutes, then stir in tomatoes right before serving.

barbecue pork pizza

PREP: 20 minutes   BAKE: 12 minutes at 425°F   MAKES: 4 servings

  2 portions Shredded Pork Base (2 cups), thawed (see recipe, page 35)
  ½ cup barbecue sauce
  2 medium red and/or yellow sweet peppers, seeded and cut into narrow strips
  1 medium onion, cut into narrow wedges
  1 tablespoon vegetable oil
  1 12-inch packaged prebaked pizza crust
  1 cup shredded Monterey Jack cheese (4 ounces)

1. Preheat oven to 425°F. In a medium bowl combine Shredded Pork Base and barbecue sauce; set aside.

2. In a large skillet cook sweet peppers and onion in hot oil over medium-high heat for 5 minutes or until vegetables are crisp-tender.

3. Place pizza crust on an ungreased baking sheet or pizza pan. Spoon meat mixture on crust. Top with vegetables; sprinkle with cheese. Bake for 12 minutes or until cheese is melted and crust is lightly browned.

Per serving: 718 cal., 33 g fat (14 g sat. fat), 93 mg chol., 1,191 mg sodium, 68 g carb., 4 g fiber, 36 g pro.

shredded pork sandwiches with vinegar slaw

PREP: 15 minutes   CHILL: 2 hours   COOK: 10 minutes   MAKES: 6 servings

- 3 **cups packaged shredded cabbage with carrot (coleslaw mix)**
- ¼ **cup cider vinegar**
- 2 **tablespoons honey**
- ¼ **teaspoon salt**
- ⅛ **teaspoon black pepper**
- 3 **portions Shredded Pork Base (3 cups), thawed (see recipe, page 35)**
- 1 **cup barbecue sauce**
- 6 **kaiser rolls or hoagie buns, split and toasted**
   Barbecue sauce (optional)
   Bottled hot pepper sauce (optional)

1. For slaw, in a medium bowl toss together coleslaw mix, vinegar, honey, salt, and pepper. Cover and chill for 2 to 24 hours, stirring occasionally.

2. In a medium saucepan combine Shredded Pork Base and the 1 cup barbecue sauce. Cook, covered, over medium heat about 10 minutes or until heated through, stirring occasionally.

3. To serve, drain slaw, discarding liquid. Divide pork among roll bottoms. Top with slaw; replace roll tops. If desired, serve with additional barbecue sauce and bottled hot pepper sauce.

Per serving: 502 cal., 19 g fat (6 g sat. fat), 68 mg chol., 1,035 mg sodium, 56 g carb., 3 g fiber, 25 g pro.

pork verde tacos

PREP: 15 minutes   COOK: 10 minutes   MAKES: 5 servings

3 portions Shredded Pork Base (3 cups)
(see recipe, page 35)
1 cup green salsa (salsa verde)
10 6-inch corn tortillas, heated according
to package directions

1 recipe Quick Jalapeño Sauce
Shredded cabbage and/or crumbled
queso fresco (optional)
Lime wedges (optional)

1. In a large saucepan combine Shredded Pork Base and green salsa. Cook, covered, over medium heat about 10 minutes or until heated through, stirring occasionally.

2. Spoon pork onto tortillas. Top with Quick Jalapeño Sauce and, if desired, cabbage and/or queso fresco. Fold tortillas over filling. If desired, serve with lime wedges.

QUICK JALAPEÑO SAUCE: In a small bowl stir together ¼ cup mayonnaise; 2 tablespoons snipped fresh cilantro; one-half of a small fresh jalapeño chile pepper, seeded and finely chopped (see tip, page 29); 1 teaspoon cider vinegar, 1 teaspoon water; and 1 small clove garlic, minced.

Per serving: *425 cal., 26 g fat (7 g sat. fat), 73 mg chol., 558 mg sodium, 25 g carb., 4 g fiber, 22 g pro.*

Make the Quick Jalapeño Sauce a few hours ahead. Cover and store in the refrigerator until serving time.

spicy pork, noodle, and plum skillet

START TO FINISH: 25 minutes   MAKES: 4 servings

    1 tablespoon vegetable oil
    1 small onion, cut into narrow wedges
    2 cloves garlic, minced
1½ cups water
    2 medium orange, red, and/or yellow sweet peppers, cut into narrow strips
    1 cup fresh sugar snap pea pods, trimmed
    1 3-ounce package pork-flavor ramen noodles, broken
    2 tablespoons plum sauce
    2 to 3 teaspoons Asian chili sauce (Sriracha sauce)
    2 portions Shredded Pork Base (2 cups), thawed (see recipe, page 35)
    2 plums, halved, pitted, and thinly sliced

1. In a large skillet heat oil over medium heat. Add onion and garlic; cook and stir for 2 minutes or until garlic is fragrant and onion has softened.

2. Add the water to skillet; bring to boiling. Add peppers, sugar snap pea pods, noodles and seasoning packet, plum sauce, and chili sauce. Return to boiling; reduce heat. Simmer, covered, for 5 minutes. Add Shredded Pork Base and plums; heat through. Serve in shallow bowls.

Per serving: *388 cal., 16 g fat (5 g sat. fat), 81 mg chol., 839 mg sodium, 29 g carb., 3 g fiber, 30 g pro.*

Buying cut-up vegetables from a supermarket salad bar—such as the sweet pepper strips in this recipe—can save prep time.

▶▶▶ grain, bean, and lentil base

MAKE AHEAD UP TO 3 MONTHS

PREP: 20 minutes   COOK: 40 minutes   MAKES: 14 1-cup portions

2	cups chopped onions
8 to 10	cloves garlic, minced
2	tablespoons butter
2	tablespoons olive oil
1¼	cups brown or yellow lentils
7	cups water
2	tablespoons dried parsley
2	bay leaves
1	teaspoon salt
½	teaspoon black pepper
1½	cups quick-cooking barley
1	cup uncooked quinoa, rinsed and drained
2	15- to 16-ounce cans cannellini (white kidney), navy, black, or garbanzo beans, rinsed and drained

1. In a 4- to 5-quart Dutch oven cook onions and garlic in hot butter and olive oil over medium heat for 10 minutes or until onions are tender, stirring occasionally.

2. Stir in the lentils, the water, parsley, bay leaves, salt, and pepper. Bring to boiling; reduce heat. Simmer, covered, for 15 minutes. Add the barley and quinoa. Return to boiling; reduce heat. Simmer, covered, about 15 minutes more or until lentils are tender. Drain off any excess liquid. Stir in the beans.

3. To store, place Grain, Bean, and Lentil Base in 2-cup portions in airtight containers or freezer containers. Cover and store in the refrigerator up to 3 days or freeze up to 3 months. If frozen, thaw in the refrigerator overnight before using.

base recipe ▶

spinach salad with pears and blue cheese

PREP: 15 minutes   MAKES: 4 servings

    3 tablespoons balsamic vinegar
    3 tablespoons olive oil
    1 tablespoon snipped fresh oregano
    1 clove garlic, minced
  ⅛ teaspoon black pepper
    1 portion Grain, Bean, and Lentil Base (2 cups), thawed (see recipe, page 51)
    6 cups fresh baby spinach
    1 pear, cored and thinly sliced
  ½ cup chopped walnuts, toasted (see tip below)
  ¼ cup crumbled blue cheese (optional)

1. For vinaigrette, in a screw-top jar combine vinegar, oil, oregano, garlic, and pepper. Cover and shake well.

2. In a large bowl toss together Grain, Bean, and Lentil Base with vinaigrette until well combined.

3. Line a large bowl or platter with spinach. Spoon Grain, Bean, and Lentil Base on the spinach. Arrange pear slices over top; sprinkle with walnuts and crumbled blue cheese, if desired.

Per serving: *354 cal., 22 g fat (3 g sat. fat), 2 mg chol., 195 mg sodium, 32 g carb., 9 g fiber, 9 g pro.*

To toast whole nuts or large pieces, spread them in a shallow pan. Bake in a 350°F oven for 5 to 10 minutes, shaking the pan once or twice. Toast coconut the same way, watching closely to avoid burning. Toast chopped or ground nuts or seeds in a skillet over medium heat, stirring often.

veggie burgers

PREP: 20 minutes   COOK: 10 minutes   MAKES: 6 servings

  2 tablespoons finely chopped carrot
  2 tablespoons finely chopped red sweet pepper
  2 tablespoons frozen whole kernel corn
  1 portion Grain, Bean, and Lentil Base (2 cups), thawed (see recipe, page 51)
  1 egg
  ½ teaspoon salt
  ½ teaspoon Cajun seasoning
  ¼ cup seasoned fine dry bread crumbs
  2 tablespoons olive oil
  6 whole grain hamburger buns, split and toasted
  ⅓ cup refrigerated avocado dip (guacamole)
  6 small Bibb lettuce leaves
  6 tomato slices

1. Place carrot, sweet pepper, corn, and 1 tablespoon water in a small microwave-safe bowl. Cover with waxed paper and microwave on 100% power (high) for 2 minutes or until tender. Drain, if necessary, and set aside.

2. Place Grain, Bean, and Lentil Base in a large bowl; coarsely mash with a potato masher or with a fork. Stir in cooked vegetables, egg, salt, and Cajun seasoning. Place crumbs in a shallow dish. Divide mixture into six portions. Press each portion firmly into a ball, then roll in bread crumbs to coat. Flatten into 2½-inch patties. Heat oil in an extra-large skillet over medium heat. Cook patties for 5 minutes per side or until browned and heated through (160°F).

3. Spread cut sides of buns with guacamole. Serve patties in buns with lettuce and tomato.

Per serving: 291 cal., 11 g fat (3 g sat. fat), 32 mg chol., 630 mg sodium, 42 g carb., 9 g fiber, 12 g pro.

TO BAKE PATTIES: Preheat oven to 400°F. Coat a baking sheet with nonstick cooking spray. Arrange patties on the baking sheet. Coat patties with cooking spray. Bake for 12 minutes or until browned and heated through, turning once during baking.

Homemade guacamole can be made a few hours ahead of serving time.
Store it in the refrigerator with plastic wrap touching the entire surface
of the dip to keep it from turning brown. Stir before using.

greek wraps

START TO FINISH: 25 minutes   MAKES: 4 servings

    6 ounces plain yogurt
   ⅓ cup crumbled feta cheese
    2 tablespoons snipped fresh chives
    1 clove garlic, minced
   ⅛ teaspoon black pepper
    2 cups fresh baby spinach
    1 portion Grain, Bean, and Lentil Base (2 cups), thawed (see recipe, page 51)
    1 cup thinly sliced cucumber
   ½ cup chopped roasted red pepper or fresh tomato
   ¼ cup pitted, chopped olives
    4 Greek pita flatbreads

1. For the yogurt sauce, in a small bowl combine yogurt, feta cheese, chives, garlic, and black pepper; set aside.

2. Divide spinach; Grain, Bean, and Lentil Base; cucumber; red pepper; and olives among flatbreads. Spoon yogurt sauce on filling; fold in half to serve.

Per serving: *402 cal., 9 g fat (3 g sat. fat), 16 mg chol., 812 mg sodium, 64 g carb., 10 g fiber, 18 g pro.*

The yogurt sauce can be made a few hours ahead of serving time. Store it in a tightly sealed container until ready to serve.

caramelized veggie skillet

START TO FINISH: 25 minutes   MAKES: 4 servings

3 tablespoons olive oil
8 ounces Brussels sprouts, rinsed, trimmed, and halved lengthwise (2 cups)
1 medium fennel bulb, trimmed, quartered, cored, and thinly sliced (1 cup)
2 carrots, sliced (1 cup)
½ teaspoon salt
¼ teaspoon black pepper
2 tablespoons water
1 portion Grain, Bean, and Lentil Base (2 cups), thawed (see recipe, page 51)
1 teaspoon finely shredded lemon peel
2 tablespoons lemon juice
2 ounces fontina cheese, shredded (½ cup)

1. In an extra-large nonstick skillet heat 2 tablespoons of the oil over medium heat. Add Brussels sprouts, cut sides down, in a single layer. Top with fennel and carrots. Drizzle with remaining olive oil and sprinkle with salt and pepper. Cover and cook for 3 minutes. Remove lid and drizzle sprouts with the water. Cover and cook for 3 minutes more or until sprouts are browned and crisp-tender.

2. Remove cover. Add the Grain, Bean, and Lentil Base to skillet then stir until combined and heated through. Stir in the lemon peel and lemon juice. Sprinkle with cheese.

Per serving: *314 cal., 17 g fat (5 g sat. fat), 19 mg chol., 596 mg sodium, 32 g carb., 10 g fiber, 11 g pro.,*

TIP

When you juice a lemon, lime or orange for a recipe, first wash the fruit and finely shred the peel. Store the peel in a bag in the freezer for future use. Keep one bag each for lemon, lime, and orange—and simply add to or take from the bags as needed.

tuscan kale soup

PREP: 25 minutes   COOK: 20 minutes   MAKES: 6 servings

1 cup coarsely chopped carrot (1 medium)
½ cup coarsely chopped celery (1 stalk)
1 tablespoon olive oil
2 links cooked sweet Italian-style chicken sausage, thinly sliced (6 ounces)
¼ teaspoon salt
4 cups reduced-sodium chicken broth
1 15-ounce can diced tomatoes
1 portion Grain, Bean, and Lentil Base (2 cups), thawed (see recipe, page 51)
4 cups torn fresh kale
1 tablespoon snipped fresh thyme
2 teaspoons snipped fresh oregano
6 tablespoons finely shredded Parmesan cheese

1. In a 4-quart Dutch oven cook carrot and celery in hot oil over medium heat for 10 minutes or just until carrot is tender. Add chicken sausage and salt; cook and stir about 4 minutes more or until sausage is lightly browned.

2. Stir in chicken broth; tomatoes; and Grain, Bean, and Lentil Base. Bring to boiling. Add kale, thyme, and oregano. Reduce heat. Simmer, uncovered, for 5 minutes. Top each serving with 1 tablespoon Parmesan cheese.

Per serving: *217 cal., 8 g fat (2 g sat. fat), 27 mg chol., 1,015 mg sodium, 23 g carb., 6 g fiber, 15 g pro.*

To save a prep step, look in the produce section of your supermarket for packaged fresh kale that has been cleaned, trimmed, and torn. Just open the package, measure, and add to the pot.

▶▶▶ shredded chicken base

MAKE AHEAD UP TO 3 MONTHS

PREP: 40 minutes   ROAST: 35 minutes at 400°F   MAKES: 8 1-cup portions

7½ to 8 pounds bone-in chicken thighs, skin removed
  ¼ cup lemon juice
  2 tablespoons olive oil
  1 teaspoon salt
  1 teaspoon dried thyme, crushed
  1 teaspoon paprika
  ½ teaspoon black pepper

1. Preheat oven to 400°F. Line two 15×10×1-inch baking pans with foil. Place chicken thighs in the prepared baking pans. Drizzle with lemon juice and oil. In a small bowl stir together salt, thyme, paprika, and pepper. Sprinkle seasoning blend over chicken.

2. Roast, uncovered, for 35 to 40 minutes or until chicken is no longer pink (180°F). Remove from oven. When chicken is cool enough to handle, remove meat from bones; discard bones. Using two forks, pull chicken apart into shreds.

3. To store, place shredded chicken in 1-cup portions in airtight containers or freezer containers. Cover and store in the refrigerator up to 3 days or freeze up to 3 months. If frozen, thaw in the refrigerator overnight before using.

▶▶ cheese sauce

MAKE AHEAD UP TO 3 DAYS

START TO FINISH: 30 minutes   MAKES: 9 1-cup portions

- ¼ cup butter
- ½ cup finely chopped onion
- 2 cloves garlic, minced
- ¼ cup all-purpose flour
- ¼ teaspoon black pepper
- 3 cups milk
- 12 ounces shredded three-cheese blend (cheddar, Colby, and Monterey Jack) with cream cheese

1. In a 2-quart Dutch oven melt butter over medium heat. Add onion and garlic; cook about 6 minutes or until onion is tender, stirring occasionally. Stir in flour and pepper; cook and stir for 1 minute. Gradually stir in milk. Cook until sauce is thickened and bubbly, stirring frequently. Gradually add cheese blend, stirring until melted.

2. Place Cheese Sauce in 1-cup portions airtight containers. Cover and store in the refrigerator up to 3 days.

base recipes▶

▶▶▶ chicken enchiladas

MAKE AHEAD UP TO 3 MONTHS

PREP: 25 minutes   BAKE: 35 minutes at 375°F   MAKES: 4 servings

- 1 15-ounce can navy beans, rinsed and drained
- 2 portions Shredded Chicken Base (2 cups), thawed (see recipe, page 62)
- 2 portions Cheese Sauce (2 cups) (see recipe, page 63)
- 1 8-ounce package shredded Mexican four-cheese blend (Monterey Jack, cheddar, asadero, and queso quesadilla) with cream cheese or shredded Monterey Jack cheese with jalapeño peppers and cream cheese (2 cups)
- 1 4-ounce can diced green chile peppers, drained
- 8 8-inch flour tortillas
  Chopped roma tomatoes, snipped fresh cilantro, and/or sour cream (optional)

1. Preheat oven to 375°F. For filling, in a medium bowl combine beans and Shredded Chicken Base. Stir in ½ cup of the Cheese Sauce, ½ cup of the cheese, and the green chile peppers.

2. To assemble enchiladas, place about ½ cup of the filling on each tortilla. Roll tortillas and place, seam sides down, in a 3-quart rectangular baking dish. (If tortillas are not pliable enough to roll easily before filling, place tortillas between paper towels and microwave on 100 percent power (high) for 20 to 40 seconds.) Top enchiladas with the remaining Cheese Sauce and sprinkle with the remaining 1½ cups cheese.

3. Bake for 35 to 40 minutes or until heated through. If necessary to prevent overbrowning, cover loosely with foil the last 10 to 20 minutes of baking. If desired, serve with chopped roma tomatoes, snipped fresh cilantro, and/or sour cream.

Per serving: *498 cal., 425 g fat (12 g sat. fat), 101 mg chol., 1,131 mg sodium, 42 g carb., 3 g fiber, 30 g pro.*

To make enchiladas ahead to freeze, cover baking dish with plastic wrap or foil, then place dish in a resealable freezer bag. Seal and freeze up to 3 months. To serve, thaw in the refrigerator overnight. Preheat oven to 375°F. Remove plastic wrap or foil and follow directions in Step 3.

individual chicken potpies

PREP: 20 minutes   BAKE: 35 minutes at 425°F   MAKES: 6 servings

- 1 **16-ounce package frozen mixed vegetables (beans, corn, carrots, and peas)**
- 3 **portions Shredded Chicken Base (3 cups), thawed (see recipe, page 62)**
- 2 **portions Cheese Sauce (2 cups) (see recipe, page 63)**
- 1 **tablespoon snipped fresh thyme**
- ½ **teaspoon black pepper**
- ¼ **teaspoon salt**
- 1 **recipe Pastry Dough (see recipe, page 29)**

1. Preheat oven to 425°F. For filling, in a large bowl combine frozen mixed vegetables, Shredded Chicken Base, Cheese Sauce, thyme, pepper, and salt. Divide filling among six 10-ounce ramekins or custard cups, or among six 5×1¼-inch individual pie pans.

2. Divide Pastry Dough into six portions. Roll each portion into a 6-inch circle. Place pastry circles on filling. Turn under edges of pastry; crimp edges as desired. Using a sharp knife, cut a small cutout or a few slits in each pastry top to allow steam to escape.

3. Place potpies on a foil-lined baking sheet. Bake for 35 minutes or until golden and bubbly.

Per serving: *794 cal., 45 g fat (19 g sat. fat), 182 mg chol., 1,075 mg sodium, 57 g carb., 5 g fiber, 40 g pro.*

chicken and cherry salad with toasted almonds

START TO FINISH: 25 minutes   MAKES: 4 servings

½ cup tart cherry preserves
3 tablespoons olive oil
2 tablespoons red wine vinegar
2 teaspoons Dijon-style mustard
1 clove garlic, minced
¼ teaspoon salt
8 cups torn romaine lettuce and/or spinach
2 portions Shredded Chicken Base (2 cups), thawed (see recipe, page 62)
1 medium red or green apple, cored and thinly sliced
½ cup shredded Monterey Jack or cheddar cheese
⅓ cup sliced almonds, toasted (see tip, page 52)
¼ cup dried tart cherries

1. For vinaigrette, in a small bowl whisk together the cherry preserves, olive oil, vinegar, mustard, garlic, and salt. (If desired, cover and chill vinaigrette up to 3 days.)

2. Divide lettuce among four dinner plates. Top with Shredded Chicken Base. Arrange apple slices on chicken. Sprinkle with cheese, almonds, and cherries. Drizzle each serving with the cherry vinaigrette.

Per serving: *531 cal., 25 g fat (6 g sat. fat), 134 mg chol., 538 mg sodium, 47 g carb., 5 g fiber, 31 g pro.*

When you bring greens such as romaine lettuce or a bunch of fresh spinach home from the supermarket, trim, wash, and spin the greens dry immediately. Store the salad spinner in the refrigerator so they are ready to use.

asian chicken and noodle bowl

PREP: 15 minutes   COOK: 5 minutes   MAKES: 2 servings

   2 cups water
   1 3-ounce package ramen noodles
   2 teaspoons vegetable oil
   1 teaspoon grated fresh ginger
   2 cloves garlic, minced
 ½ cup chicken broth
   1 tablespoon soy sauce
   1 portion Shredded Chicken Base (1 cup), thawed (see recipe, page 62)
1½ cups torn fresh spinach
 ½ cup shredded carrots
 ¼ cup fresh cilantro leaves
   1 teaspoon Sriracha sauce
 ¼ cup chopped peanuts (optional)

1. In a medium saucepan bring the water to boiling. If desired, break up noodles; drop noodles into the boiling water. (Reserve flavor packet for another use.) Return to boiling; boil for 2 to 3 minutes or just until noodles are tender but firm, stirring occasionally. Drain noodles.

2. Pour oil into a wok or large skillet. Preheat over medium-high heat. Stir-fry ginger and garlic in hot oil for 30 seconds. Add chicken broth and soy sauce. Bring to boiling. Reduce heat and stir Shredded Chicken Base into broth mixture. Cook and stir 1 to 2 minutes or until heated through.

3. Add noodles, spinach, carrots, cilantro, and Sriracha sauce to mixture in wok; toss to combine. Ladle into soup bowls. If desired, sprinkle with peanuts.

Per serving: 434 cal., 19 g fat (5 g sat. fat), 122 mg chol., 1,151 mg sodium, 34 g carb., 3 g fiber, 32 g pro.

creamy masala chicken

PREP: 20 minutes   COOK: 10 minutes   MAKES: 4 servings

    2 tablespoons vegetable oil
    4 cloves garlic, minced
    1 tablespoon grated fresh ginger
    1 fresh jalapeño chile pepper, seeded and finely chopped (see tip, page 29)
    1 shallot, finely chopped
    1 teaspoon garam masala
    ½ teaspoon sweet smoked paprika
    ¼ teaspoon salt
    2 14.5-ounce cans fire-roasted tomatoes
    ⅔ cup whipping cream
    2 portions Shredded Chicken Base (2 cups), thawed (see tip, page 62)
    1 10-ounce package frozen peas, thawed
    3 cups hot cooked basmati rice
      Fresh cilantro leaves

1. For masala sauce, in a large saucepan heat the oil over medium-high heat. Add the garlic, ginger, jalapeño pepper, and shallot; cook, stirring occasionally, for 3 minutes. Stir in the garam masala, paprika, and salt. Cook and stir for 30 seconds. Stir in the tomatoes, scraping up any browned bits. Remove saucepan from heat; cool slightly.

2. Transfer the sauce to a blender or food processor. Cover and blend until smooth. Return sauce to the pan; stir in the cream, Shredded Chicken Base, and peas. Heat through, stirring occasionally (do not boil).

3. Divide cooked rice among bowls then top with Creamy Chicken Masala. Sprinkle with cilantro.

Per serving: *633 cal., 29 g fat (11 g sat. fat), 176 mg chol., 935 mg sodium, 60 g carb., 5 g fiber, 34 g pro.*

Next time you cook rice, make a double batch and freeze the leftovers. Rice reheats perfectly in the microwave. Cool extra rice completely in the refrigerator so the grains stay separate, then freeze portions in bags labeled with the amount, date, and type of rice.

chicken potato chowder

PREP: 20 minutes   HEAT: 10 minutes   MAKES: 6 servings

  2 **14.5-ounce cans chicken broth**
  3 **cups frozen diced hash brown potatoes**
  2 **portions Cheese Sauce (2 cups) (see recipe, page 63)**
  2 **portions Shredded Chicken Base (2 cups), thawed (see recipe, page 62)**
  ½ **cup frozen peas with pearl onions**
  ½ **cup frozen whole kernel corn**
  1 **cup shredded cheddar cheese (4 ounces)**
     Coarsely crumbled, crisp-cooked bacon and/or snipped fresh Italian (flat-leaf) parsley (optional)

1. In a Dutch oven combine chicken broth, hash brown potatoes, Cheese Sauce, Shredded Chicken Base, peas, and corn. Cook over medium-low heat about 10 minutes or until heated through, stirring occasionally. If desired, mash potatoes slightly with a potato masher.

2. To serve, sprinkle servings with cheddar cheese and, if desired, sprinkle with bacon and/or parsley.

Per serving: 440 cal., 23 g fat (13 g sat. fat), 121 mg chol., 1,065 mg sodium, 30 g carb., 2 g fiber, 28 g pro.

barbecue chicken stromboli

PREP: 30 minutes   RISE: 8 hours or overnight   BAKE: 30 minutes at 375°F   MAKES: 6 servings

1 recipe Pizza Dough, thawed if frozen (see recipe, page 26)
2 portions Shredded Chicken Base (2 cups), thawed (see recipe, page 62)
¾ cup barbecue sauce
⅓ cup chopped red onion
⅓ cup chopped green sweet pepper
2 tablespoons chopped sweet pickles or banana peppers (optional)
2 cups shredded Monterey Jack cheese with jalapeño peppers (8 ounces)
1 egg, lightly beaten
1 tablespoon water

1. Line a large baking sheet with parchment paper; set aside. Roll each portion of Pizza Dough into a 12×10-inch rectangle.

2. For filling, in a medium bowl combine Shredded Chicken Base, barbecue sauce, red onion, sweet pepper, and, if desired, pickles. Spread filling on dough to within 1 inch of the edges. Sprinkle with cheese. In a small bowl combine egg and the water; brush some of the egg mixture on edges of dough. Roll up each rectangle, starting from a long side; pinch dough to seal seams and ends.

3. Place loaves, seam sides down, on the prepared baking sheet. Brush with the remaining egg mixture. Cover loosely with plastic wrap. Let rise in the refrigerator overnight.

4. Preheat oven to 375°F. Remove plastic wrap from loaves. Using a sharp knife, cut a few slits in tops of loaves for steam to escape. Bake for 30 to 35 minutes or until golden. Cool slightly. Cut loaves into slices.

Per serving: *564 cal., 22 g fat (9 g sat. fat), 148 mg chol., 971 mg sodium, 56 g carb., 2 g fiber, 31 g pro.*

QUICK

▶▶▶ cajun pasta

MAKE AHEAD UP TO 2 MONTHS

PREP: 30 minutes   BAKE: 1 hour 15 minutes at 350°F   STAND: 15 minutes   MAKES: 6 servings

  6 ounces dried bow tie pasta
  2 portions Cheese Sauce (2 cups) (see recipe, page 63)
  2 portions Shredded Chicken Base (2 cups), thawed (see recipe, page 62)
  1 cup frozen sweet pepper and onion stir-fry vegetables
  ½ cup milk
  ⅓ cup chopped roma tomato (1 medium)
1½ teaspoons Cajun seasoning
  2 cloves garlic, minced
  1 teaspoon bottled hot pepper sauce
  ½ teaspoon dried thyme, crushed
  ⅔ cup panko bread crumbs
  3 slices bacon, crisp-cooked, drained, and crumbled
  1 clove garlic
  ¼ teaspoon paprika
  1 cup shredded cheddar and Monterey Jack cheese (4 ounces)

1. Preheat oven to 350°F. Cook pasta according to package directions; drain. Rinse with cold water until cool; drain again. In a large bowl combine cooked pasta, Cheese Sauce, Shredded Chicken Base, frozen stir-fry vegetables, milk, tomato, Cajun seasoning, 2 cloves minced garlic, hot pepper sauce, and thyme. Transfer pasta mixture to a 2-quart rectangular baking dish or an 8×8×1⅞-inch disposable foil baking pan.

2. For crumb topping, in a food processor or blender combine panko, bacon, 1 clove garlic, and paprika. Cover and process or blend with on/off pulses until fine crumbs form. Sprinkle shredded cheese and crumb topping on casserole.

3. Bake, covered, for 1 hour. Uncover and bake 15 minutes more or until heated through and golden. Let stand 15 minutes before serving.

Per serving: *496 cal., 25 g fat (13 g sat. fat), 127 mg chol., 641 mg sodium, 35 g carb., 2 g fiber, 31 g pro.*

To make and freeze Cajun Pasta, cover baking dish with foil. Place the dish in a resealable freezer bag. Seal and freeze up to 2 months. To serve, thaw in the refrigerator overnight (casserole may still be a bit icy). Preheat oven to 350°F then follow directions in Step 3.

FROM THE
freezer ▶

These satisfying casseroles, soups, stews, sandwiches, and stuffed pizzas are the best frozen assets. Just thaw, heat, and eat.

recipes ▶▶▶ WEEKS OR MONTHS AHEAD

▶▶▶ beef and barley stew with roasted winter vegetables

MAKE AHEAD UP TO 2 MONTHS

PREP: 45 minutes   COOK: 1 hour 35 minutes   ROAST: 35 minutes at 375°F
FREEZE: up to 2 months   THAW: 1 to 2 days   MAKES: 6 servings

- ¼ cup all-purpose flour
- ½ teaspoon salt
- ½ teaspoon black pepper
- 2 to 2½ pounds boneless beef chuck roast, trimmed of excess fat and cut into 1-inch pieces
- ¼ cup olive oil
- ½ cup chopped onion (1 medium)
- 2 cloves garlic, minced
- ½ teaspoon dried thyme, crushed
- 1 14.5-ounce can beef broth

- 2 cups water
- 1 cup dry red wine
- 4 medium red or yellow potatoes and/or sweet potatoes, cut into 1-inch chunks
- 4 medium carrots and/or parsnips, peeled and cut into 1-inch chunks
- ½ cup regular barley
  Beef broth (optional)
- 2 tablespoons snipped fresh Italian (flat-leaf) parsley (optional)

1. In a large bowl combine flour, ¼ teaspoon of the salt, and ¼ teaspoon of the pepper. Add meat; toss to coat. In a Dutch oven heat 1 tablespoon of the olive oil over medium heat. Add half the meat; cook until browned, stirring occasionally. Remove meat from Dutch oven; set aside. Repeat with another 1 tablespoon of the oil and the remaining meat.

2. Add onion, garlic, and thyme to Dutch oven. Cook and stir for 3 minutes. Add the can of broth, stirring to scrape up any browned bits from bottom of the Dutch oven. Add the water and wine. Bring to boiling; reduce heat to low. Simmer, covered, for 1 hour.

3. Meanwhile, preheat oven to 375°F. In a shallow roasting pan combine potatoes and carrots and/or parsnips. Drizzle with the remaining 2 tablespoons olive oil; sprinkle with the remaining ¼ teaspoon salt and the remaining ¼ teaspoon pepper. Toss to coat. Roast, uncovered, for 35 to 45 minutes or until vegetables are tender and lightly browned, stirring once or twice.

4. Stir barley into beef mixture. Cook for 35 minutes more or until barley is tender. Stir in roasted vegetables. Serve in shallow bowls; sprinkle with parsley, if desired.

5. To store stew, cool stew slightly and transfer to freezer containers. Cover and freeze for up to 2 months. To serve, thaw stew in refrigerator for 1 to 2 days. Place thawed stew in a Dutch oven and heat over medium heat until bubbly, stirring occasionally. Stir in additional beef broth, if necessary, to reach desired consistency. If desired, stir in fresh parsley.

Per serving: 455 cal., 24 g fat (8 g sat. fat), 71 mg chol., 436 mg sodium, 27 g carb., 5 g fiber, 26 g pro.

TIP

To refrigerate rather than freeze stew, follow directions through Step 4. Cool stew slightly then transfer to an airtight container. Cover and refrigerate up to 3 days. To serve, continue as directed in Step 5.

▶▶▶ italian beef sandwiches

MAKE AHEAD UP TO 1 MONTH

PREP: 20 minutes   FREEZE: up to 1 month   THAW: 30 minutes
ROAST: 3 hours at 325°F   BROIL: 3 minutes   MAKES: 12 servings

- 1 **4-pound boneless beef sirloin or rump roast, cut into 2- to 3-inch pieces**
- 1 **0.7-ounce envelope Italian dry salad dressing mix**
- 2 **teaspoons dried Italian seasoning, crushed**
- 1 **teaspoon garlic powder**
- ½ **to 1 teaspoon crushed red pepper**
- ½ **cup water**
- 12 **hoagie rolls, split**
  Roasted red sweet pepper strips (optional)
  Shredded provolone cheese (optional)

1. Trim fat from meat. In a large bowl combine beef, Italian dry salad dressing mix, Italian seasoning, garlic powder, and crushed red pepper. Place seasoned beef in a large resealable plastic freezer bag or freezer container. Freeze up to 1 month. (If using a freezer bag, lay bag flat in the freezer.)

2. To serve, let frozen seasoned beef stand at room temperature for 30 minutes. Preheat oven to 325°F. Transfer seasoned beef to a 13×9×2-inch baking pan. Drizzle with the ½ cup water. Cover with foil. Roast for 3 hours or until meat is tender. Remove meat with a slotted spoon. Using two forks, shred the meat; drizzle with some of the pan juices to moisten. Place meat on rolls. If desired, top meat with roasted red pepper strips and shredded provolone cheese. Place on a foil-lined baking sheet. Broil 4 to 5 inches from the heat for 3 to 5 minutes or until cheese is melted.

Per serving: 392 cal., 8 g fat (2 g sat. fat), 91 mg chol., 677 mg sodium, 36 g carb., 2 g fiber, 41 g pro.

Label everything you store in the freezer. Include the use-by date, as well
as the quantity or number of servings.

▶▶▶ texas chili

MAKE AHEAD UP TO 2 MONTHS

PREP: 25 minutes   COOK: 2 hours   FREEZE: up to 2 months
THAW: 1 to 2 days   HEAT: 25 minutes   MAKES: 6 servings

  2 pounds boneless beef tri-tip steak (bottom sirloin) or chuck roast
  1 cup chopped onion (1 large)
¾ cup chopped green sweet pepper (1 medium)
  1 clove garlic, minced
  2 tablespoons vegetable oil
  2 14.5-ounce cans 50% less sodium beef broth
1½ to 2 cups water
  2 6-ounce cans no-salt-added tomato paste
  2 fresh jalapeño chile peppers, seeded and finely chopped (see tip, page 29)
4½ teaspoons chili powder
½ teaspoon dried oregano, crushed
½ teaspoon ground cumin
½ teaspoon crushed red pepper
  1 15-ounce can pinto beans, rinsed and drained

1. Trim fat from meat. Cut meat into ½- to ¾-inch pieces. In a 4-quart Dutch oven cook meat, onion, sweet pepper, and garlic in hot oil over medium-high heat until meat is browned and vegetables are tender, stirring frequently. Drain off fat.

2. Stir in broth, the water, tomato paste, jalapeño peppers, chili powder, oregano, cumin, and crushed red pepper. Bring to boiling; reduce heat. Simmer, covered, for 1½ hours. Stir in beans. Simmer, covered, for 30 minutes more or until meat is tender. (Serve immediately or cool slightly to store.)

3. Transfer cooled chili to freezer containers. Seal and freeze up to 2 months.

4. To serve, thaw chili in the refrigerator for 1 to 2 days. Transfer thawed chili to a 4-quart Dutch oven. Cook, stirring occasionally, over medium heat about 25 minutes or until heated through.

Per serving: 424 cal., 18 g fat (5 g sat. fat), 99 mg chol., 648 mg sodium, 27 g carb., 8 g fiber, 40 g pro.

To refrigerate rather than freeze chili, follow directions through Step 3. Cool chili slightly and transfer to an airtight container. Cover and refrigerate up to 3 days. To serve, continue as directed in Step 4.

▶▶▶ brown sugar-glazed home-style meat loaf

MAKE AHEAD UP TO 2 MONTHS

PREP: 20 minutes   FREEZE: up to 2 months   THAW: 30 minutes
BAKE: 1 hour at 350°F   STAND: 10 minutes   MAKES: 4 servings per loaf

½ cup refrigerated or frozen egg product, thawed
⅓ cup milk
⅔ cup ketchup
3 teaspoons yellow mustard
2 pounds lean ground beef
½ cup quick-cooking rolled oats
⅓ cup finely chopped onion
1 teaspoon salt
½ teaspoon black pepper
3 tablespoons packed brown sugar

1. In a large bowl combine egg product, milk, ⅓ cup of the ketchup, and 1 teaspoon of the mustard. Stir in ground beef, oats, onion, salt, and pepper; mix well. Divide and gently press meat into two ungreased 8×4×2-inch loaf pans or two 8×4×2-inch disposable foil loaf pans. Cover pans with foil. Place in large resealable plastic bags. Freeze up to 2 months. For glaze, in a small bowl combine the remaining ⅓ cup ketchup, the brown sugar, and the remaining 2 teaspoons yellow mustard. Divide among two small freezer containers. Freeze up to 2 months.

2. To serve four, remove one loaf pan and one container of glaze from freezer. Let stand at room temperature for 30 minutes. Preheat oven to 350°F. Bake, covered, for 45 minutes. Drain off fat and lightly pat top of meat loaf with paper towels. Evenly spoon glaze over meat loaf. Bake, uncovered, for 15 minutes more or until an instant-read thermometer registers 160°F. Let the meat loaf stand for 10 minutes. Carefully slice meat loaf; use a spatula to transfer to a serving platter.

Per serving: 277 cal., 12 g fat (5 g sat. fat), 75 mg chol., 604 mg sodium, 15 g carb., 1 g fiber, 26 g pro.

TIP

One meat loaf serves four people. To serve more than four, bake both loaves at the same time. If you have leftovers, make meat loaf sandwiches for lunch the next day.

▶▶▶ veggie-filled burgers

MAKE AHEAD UP TO 3 MONTHS

PREP: 25 minutes   FREEZE: up to 3 months   THAW: 12 hours   GRILL: 11 minutes
MAKES: 4 servings

- 2 tablespoons fat-free milk
- ½ cup finely shredded carrot (1 medium)
- ¼ cup thinly sliced green onions (2)
- ¼ cup soft whole wheat bread crumbs
- ¼ teaspoon garlic salt
- ¼ teaspoon dried Italian seasoning, crushed
  Dash black pepper
- 12 ounces extra-lean ground beef or uncooked ground turkey breast or chicken breast

- ¼ cup Dijon-style mustard
- ½ teaspoon curry powder
- 4 lettuce leaves
- 4 to 8 slices tomato
- ½ cup sliced zucchini
- 4 whole wheat hamburger buns, split and toasted

1. In a medium bowl stir together milk, carrot, green onions, bread crumbs, garlic salt, Italian seasoning, and pepper. Add the ground meat; mix well. Divide meat mixture into four portions. Shape each portion into a ½-inch-thick patty.

2. Grill to serve immediately, or place patties in a single layer in a freezer container. Cover and freeze up to 3 months.

3. To serve, thaw frozen patties in the refrigerator overnight. For a gas or charcoal grill, place thawed patties on the grill rack directly over medium heat. Cover and grill for 11 to 14 minutes or until an instant-read thermometer inserted into the side of each patty registers 160°F for beef or 165°F for turkey or chicken, turning once halfway through grilling.

4. Meanwhile, for curry mustard, in a small bowl combine mustard and curry powder. Spread bottoms of buns with curry mustard. Top with patties, lettuce leaves, tomato, zucchini slices, and add bun tops.

Per serving: *254 cal., 6 g fat (2 g sat. fat), 53 mg chol., 359 mg sodium, 27 g carb., 3 g fiber, 24 g pro.*

TIP

To avoid freezer burn, seal airtight containers and packages securely—
cold air dries the surface of cold food.

▶▶▶ pizza slab pie

MAKE AHEAD UP TO 1 MONTH

PREP: 25 minutes   FREEZE: up to 1 month   BAKE: 47 minutes at 375°F   MAKES: 8 servings

2 13.8-ounce packages refrigerated pizza dough

8 ounces bulk hot or sweet Italian sausage, cooked and drained

½ of a 10-ounce package frozen chopped spinach, thawed and squeezed dry

1 cup pizza sauce or pasta sauce

1 cup thawed and quartered frozen artichoke hearts

½ cup sliced pitted ripe olives or Kalamata olives

⅓ cup slivered red onion

2 cups shredded Italian cheese blend (8 ounces)

¾ cup shredded Parmesan cheese (3 ounces)

1. Preheat oven to 375°F. Lightly grease a 15×10×1-inch baking pan; set aside. Unroll one package of pizza dough on a lightly floured surface. Roll dough into a 15×10-inch rectangle. Transfer to the prepared baking pan; press edges of dough up sides of pan. Bake for 7 to 10 minutes or until light brown.

2. For filling, in a medium bowl combine sausage, spinach, pizza sauce, artichoke hearts, olives, and red onion. Spread evenly over crust in pan. Sprinkle with Italian cheese blend. (To serve today, preheat oven to 400°F. Continue, beginning with Step 4, at baking uncovered, 25 minutes, and proceeding through Step 6).

3. To freeze, cover with foil. Freeze for up to 1 month.

4. To serve, do not thaw pizza. Preheat oven to 375°F. Bake, uncovered, for 25 minutes, covering with foil the last 5 to 10 minutes if necessary to prevent overbrowning.

5. Unroll the remaining package of pizza dough. Cut dough in long strips or random-size pieces; place on filling. Sprinkle with Parmesan cheese.

6. Bake, uncovered, for 15 minutes more or until crust is golden and filling is heated through.

Per serving: 430 cal., 21 g fat (9 g sat. fat), 45 mg chol., 1,313 mg sodium, 53 g carb., 4 g fiber, 23 g pro.

To discourage ice crystals from forming on frozen food, let all cooked foods cool completely before wrapping or packaging to freeze.

▶▶▶ carnitas

MAKE AHEAD UP TO 1 MONTH

PREP: 30 minutes   COOK: 2½ hours   FREEZE: up to 1 month
THAW: 1 to 2 days   HEAT: 20 minutes   MAKES: 12 servings

- 3 pounds boneless pork shoulder roast
- 2 tablespoons lard or vegetable oil
- ⅓ cup chopped onion (1 small)
- 3 cloves garlic, minced
- 2 cups water
- 1 teaspoon finely shredded orange peel
- ⅓ cup orange juice
- 4 sprigs fresh thyme
- 2 bay leaves
- 1 teaspoon salt
- 1 teaspoon dried Mexican oregano or regular oregano, crushed
- ½ teaspoon crushed red pepper
  Flour torillas, guacamole, sliced jalapeños (see tip, page 29), lime wedges, and/or red onion relish

1. Trim fat from meat. Cut meat into 1½-inch pieces. In a Dutch oven cook meat, half at a time, in hot lard over medium-high heat until browned. Remove meat from Dutch oven. Add onion and garlic to Dutch oven; cook until tender and light brown, stirring occasionally. Return all of meat to Dutch oven. Add the water, orange peel, orange juice, thyme, bay leaves, salt, oregano, and crushed red pepper.

2. Bring to boiling; reduce heat. Simmer, covered, for 2 hours. Simmer, uncovered, for 30 to 40 minutes more or until nearly all of the liquid is evaporated, gently stirring occasionally. Remove and discard thyme sprigs and bay leaves. (To serve today, continue with Step 5.)

3. To freeze for storing, cool meat slightly then transfer it to a freezer container. Seal and freeze up to 1 month.

4. To serve, thaw meat in the refrigerator for 1 to 2 days. Transfer thawed meat to a large saucepan. Cook over medium heat for 20 minutes or until heated through, stirring occasionally.

5. Using a slotted spoon, transfer meat to a serving bowl. If desired, serve with tortillas, guacamole, sliced jalapeños, lime wedges, and/or red onion relish.

Per serving: 237 cal., 16 g fat (6 g sat. fat), 72 mg chol., 265 mg sodium, 1 g carb., 4 g fiber, 20 g pro.

TIP

To refrigerate rather than freeze carnitas, follow directions through Step 2. Cool meat slightly then transfer it to an airtight container. Cover and refrigerate up to 3 days. To serve, continue as directed in Steps 4 and 5.

▶▶▶ ham, cheese, and turkey stromboli

MAKE AHEAD UP TO 1 MONTH

PREP: 20 minutes   BAKE: 30 minutes at 375°F/35 minutes at 350°F
FREEZE: up to 1 month   THAW: 12 hours   MAKES: 4 servings

- 1 teaspoon olive oil
- 1 tablespoon cornmeal
- 1 13.8-ounce package refrigerated pizza dough
- 4 ounces thinly sliced cooked ham
- 1 cup shredded mozzarella cheese (4 ounces)
- 1 cup fresh baby spinach or torn spinach leaves
- 4 ounces thinly sliced cooked turkey
- ⅓ cup chopped red, green, or yellow sweet pepper
- ¼ cup Kalamata olives, pitted and chopped
- 1 egg, lightly beaten
  Marinara sauce or pizza sauce (optional)

1. Preheat oven to 375°F. Lightly brush a baking sheet with oil; sprinkle with cornmeal. Set aside. On a lightly floured surface, carefully stretch or roll pizza dough into a 13×10-inch rectangle. Arrange ham slices on dough to within ½ inch of the edges. Sprinkle with ½ cup of the cheese. Layer spinach and turkey on cheese. Top with the remaining ½ cup cheese, the sweet pepper, and olives. Roll dough around filling, starting from a long side; pinch dough to seal seam and ends.

2. Place loaf, seam side down, on the prepared baking sheet. Brush with beaten egg. Using a sharp knife, cut a few slits in top for steam to escape. Bake for 30 minutes or until golden. Cool slightly. (To serve today, continue as directed in Step 5.)

3. To freeze to store, transfer loaf to a wire rack; cool completely. Transfer to a resealable freezer bag or a freezer container. Seal and freeze up to 1 month.

4. To serve, thaw in the refrigerator overnight (loaf may still be a bit icy). Preheat oven to 350°F. Lightly grease a baking sheet. Transfer stromboli to the prepared baking sheet. Bake, uncovered, for 35 minutes or until heated through. Cool slightly.

5. Slice loaf into serving-size pieces. If desired, serve with marinara sauce.

Per serving: 417 cal., 17 g fat (5 g sat. fat), 93 mg chol., 1,290 mg sodium, 44 g carb., 3 g fiber, 23 g pro.

To refrigerate rather than freeze stromboli, cool stromboli as in Step 3. Transfer to a resealable plastic bag or airtight container. Seal and refrigerate for 2 to 24 hours. To serve, continue as directed in Steps 4 and 5 except bake, uncovered, for 20 minutes or until heated through.

▶▶▶ spicy sausage, mushroom, and polenta bake

MAKE AHEAD UP TO 1 MONTH

PREP: 50 minutes   FREEZE: up to 1 month   THAW: 12 hours   BAKE: 1 hour 30 minutes at 350°F
STAND: 10 minutes   MAKES: 8 servings

1 pound bulk Italian sausage
1 medium fresh jalapeño chile pepper, seeded and finely chopped (see tip, page 29) (optional)
4 cloves garlic, minced
1 24-ounce jar marinara sauce
1 tablespoon olive oil
4 cups chopped fresh mushrooms
¾ cup thinly sliced green onions (6)
1 teaspoon snipped fresh rosemary

½ cup whipping cream
¼ cup dry white wine or chicken broth
½ teaspoon salt
4 cups chicken broth
½ cup water
2 teaspoons dried Italian seasoning, crushed
1½ cups cornmeal
2 cups shredded smoked provolone cheese (8 ounces)

1. In a large skillet cook sausage, jalapeño pepper (if desired), and half the garlic over medium-high heat until meat is browned, using a wooden spoon to break up meat as it cooks. Drain off fat. Stir in marinara sauce. Bring to boiling; reduce heat. Simmer, uncovered, for 15 minutes, stirring frequently.

2. In another large skillet heat oil over medium heat. Add mushrooms, green onions, rosemary, and the remaining garlic. Cook about 5 minutes or until mushrooms are tender and liquid is evaporated, stirring occasionally. Stir in whipping cream, wine, and salt. Cook over low heat about 10 minutes or until mushroom mixture is thickened, stirring occasionally.

3. For polenta, in a large saucepan bring broth, the water, and Italian seasoning to boiling. Slowly add cornmeal, stirring constantly. Cook and stir until cornmeal mixture returns to boiling; reduce heat to low. Cook for 8 to 10 minutes or until polenta is thickened, stirring occasionally.

4. Grease a 3-quart rectangular baking dish. Spread half the sausage mixture in the prepared baking dish. Working quickly, spread half the polenta over sausage layer. Top with mushroom mixture and 1 cup of the cheese. Quickly spread the remaining polenta on cheese. Top with the remaining sausage mixture and the remaining 1 cup cheese. (To serve today, continue as directed in Step 6, except bake, covered, for 25 to 30 minutes.)

5. To freeze to store, cool completely. Then cover baking dish with plastic wrap, then with foil. Freeze for up to 1 month.

6. To serve, thaw in the refrigerator overnight (casserole may still be a bit icy). Preheat oven to 350°F. Remove plastic wrap; cover with greased foil. Bake for 1½ hours or until heated through. Let stand for 10 minutes before serving.

Per serving: 495 cal., 30 g fat (14 g sat. fat), 83 mg chol., 1,504 mg sodium, 32 g carb., 3 g fiber, 21 g pro.

▶▶▶ marinated apple-sage braised pork shoulder

MAKE AHEAD UP TO 1 MONTH

PREP: 30 minutes   FREEZE: up to 1 month   THAW: 30 minutes
BAKE: 2 hours at 325°F   MAKES: 6 servings

- 1 2½- to 3-pound boneless pork shoulder roast, trimmed and cut into 6 pieces
  Salt and black pepper
- 2 small onions, cut into wedges
- 1 tablespoon dried sage, crushed
- 2 cloves garlic, minced
- ½ cup frozen apple juice concentrate, thawed
- 8 carrots, cut into 3-inch pieces
- 3 stalks celery, cut into 2-inch pieces
  Water or chicken broth
- 2 tablespoons all-purpose flour
  Mashed Yukon gold potatoes (optional)

1. Season the pork with salt and pepper. Place meat and onions in a large resealable plastic freezer bag or container. Sprinkle sage and garlic over meat in bag. Pour apple juice concentrate over pork. Seal bag, turn to coat so marinade is equally distributed over the pork. Freeze up to 1 month.

2. To serve, let frozen bag stand at room temperature for 30 minutes. Preheat oven to 325°F. Place meat and marinade in a shallow roasting pan; add carrots and celery. Cover pan with foil. Bake for 2 to 2½ hours or until meat and vegetables are tender.

3. With a slotted spoon, transfer the pork and vegetables to a serving platter. For gravy, transfer pan drippings to a glass measuring cup. Skim off fat. Add enough water or broth to drippings to equal 1 cup. Return drippings to roasting pan. In a small bowl stir together flour and 2 tablespoons water. Add to drippings in roasting pan. Place roasting pan on the stovetop over medium heat. Cook and stir until thickened and bubbly, scraping up any browned bits. Cook and stir 2 minutes more. Strain gravy, if desired. Serve with pork, vegetables, and, if desired, mashed potatoes.

Per serving: 340 cal., 11 g fat (4 g sat. fat), 113 mg chol., 300 mg sodium, 22 g carb., 3 g fiber, 37 g pro.

Not all plastic food wraps are equal. For safe freezing, choose wraps, containers, and bags labeled specifically for freezer use.

▶▶▶ pork and sweet potato empanadas

MAKE AHEAD UP TO 6 MONTHS

PREP: 55 minutes   FREEZE: up to 6 months   THAW: 12 hours   BAKE: 20 minutes at 425°F
MAKES: 8 servings

1½ cups chopped, peeled sweet potato (1 large)	3 cups chopped cooked pork
1 8-ounce can tomato sauce	3 cups all-purpose flour
¼ cup raisins	½ teaspoon salt
1 teaspoon ground pasilla chile pepper or ancho chile pepper	½ cup shortening
½ teaspoon dry mustard	¼ cup butter
½ teaspoon ground cumin	2 eggs
¼ teaspoon salt	½ cup milk
	Milk (optional)
	1 tablespoon water

1. For filling, in a large skillet combine sweet potato, tomato sauce, raisins, ground chile pepper, dry mustard, cumin, and the ¼ teaspoon salt. Bring to boiling; reduce heat. Simmer, covered, for 10 to 12 minutes or until sweet potato is tender, stirring occasionally. Stir in pork.

2. For pastry, in a large bowl stir together flour and the ½ teaspoon salt. Using a pastry blender, cut in shortening and butter until flour mixture resembles coarse crumbs. In a small bowl lightly beat one of the eggs with a fork. Stir in ½ cup milk. Add milk mixture all at once to flour mixture; stir until combined. If dough seems dry, add enough additional milk (1 to 2 tablespoons) to make a dough that is easy to handle.

3. Turn dough out onto a lightly floured surface. Shape into a ball; divide into eight portions. Roll each portion into a 6-inch circle. Place about ½ cup of the filling in the center of each circle. Brush edges of circles with additional milk; fold circles in half. Pinch edges or press with a fork to seal. (To serve today, place filled empanadas on an ungreased baking sheet. Continue as directed in Step 6.)

4. To freeze empanadas, place filled empanadas on a baking sheet lined with waxed paper, then freeze about 2 hours or until firm. Transfer empanadas to a resealable freezer bag or a freezer container. Seal and freeze up to 6 months.

5. To serve, transfer frozen empanadas to an ungreased baking sheet. Thaw in the refrigerator overnight.

6. Preheat oven to 425°F. In a small bowl combine the remaining egg and the water; brush over empanadas. Prick tops with the tines of a fork. Bake for 20 minutes or until golden and heated through.

Per serving: *516 cal., 25 g fat (9 g sat. fat), 111 mg chol., 489 mg sodium, 47 g carb., 3 g fiber, 24 g pro.*

These Spanish-style stuffed pastries are a terrific way to make good use of leftover pork shoulder from a large roast.

▶▶▶ spicy pork tenderloin green chili

MAKE AHEAD UP TO 2 MONTHS

PREP: 45 minutes   ROAST: 20 minutes at 425°F   STAND: 15 minutes   COOK: 20 minutes
FREEZE: up to 2 months   THAW: 1 to 2 days   HEAT: 30 minutes   MAKES: 6 servings

      3 to 4 fresh Anaheim chile peppers (8 ounces), halved lengthwise, stems and membranes removed (see tip, page 29)
 1½ pounds pork tenderloin
      2 tablespoons canola oil
      3 cups chopped onions (3 large)
      3 tablespoons bottled minced garlic
      1 pound fresh tomatillos, peeled and chopped (about 4 cups)
      1 tablespoon ground cumin
      2 teaspoons dried oregano, crushed
      3 cups reduced-sodium chicken broth
      1 cup water
      1 15-ounce can no-salt-added navy beans, rinsed and drained
      1 tablespoon lime juice
      2 tablespoons snipped fresh cilantro

1. Preheat oven to 425°F. Place pepper halves, cut sides down, on a foil-lined baking sheet. Roast for 20 to 25 minutes or until peppers are charred and very tender. Bring foil up around peppers and fold edges together to enclose. Let stand for 15 minutes or until cool enough to handle. Using a sharp knife, carefully remove and discard skins; chop peppers. Set aside.

2. Meanwhile, trim fat from meat. Cut meat into ¾-inch pieces. In a 5- to 6-quart Dutch oven cook meat in hot oil over medium-high heat until browned. Add onions and garlic; cook for 5 minutes more or just until onions are tender, stirring occasionally. Add tomatillos, cumin, and oregano; cook for 3 minutes more, stirring occasionally.

3. Stir in broth and the water. Bring to boiling; reduce heat. Simmer, uncovered, for 15 minutes, stirring occasionally. Stir in beans, lime juice, and chopped peppers. Simmer, uncovered, for 5 minutes more. (To serve today, sprinkle each serving with cilantro.)

4. Cool chili slightly then transfer to freezer containers. Cover and freeze up to 2 months.

5. Thaw chili in the refrigerator for 1 to 2 days. To serve, transfer thawed or chilled chili to a 5- to 6-quart Dutch oven. Cook over medium heat for 30 minutes or until heated through, stirring occasionally. Sprinkle each serving with cilantro.

Per serving: *304 cal., 8 g fat (1 g sat. fat), 74 mg chol., 364 mg sodium, 26 g carb., 10 g fiber, 32 g pro.*

To refrigerate rather than freeze chili, follow directions through Step 3. Cool chili slightly then transfer to airtight containers. Cover and refrigerate up to 3 days. To serve, continue as directed in Step 5.

▶▶▶ two-pea soup with pork

MAKE AHEAD UP TO 2 MONTHS

PREP: 30 minutes   ROAST: 15 minutes at 425°F   COOK: 45 minutes
FREEZE: up to 2 months   THAW: 1 to 2 days   HEAT: 25 minutes   MAKES: 6 servings

2 medium carrots, cut into 1-inch pieces	½ teaspoon dried summer savory or marjoram, crushed
2 stalks celery, cut into 1-inch pieces	¼ teaspoon black pepper
1 large onion, cut into wedges	1 16-ounce package frozen green peas
3 cloves garlic, peeled	⅓ cup packed fresh Italian (flat-leaf) parsley leaves
1 tablespoon olive oil	2 tablespoons lemon juice
6 cups water	Salt
2 pounds meaty smoked pork hocks	Black pepper
1 cup dry split peas, rinsed and drained	

1. Preheat oven to 425°F. In a shallow baking pan combine carrots, celery, onion, and garlic. Drizzle with oil; toss gently to coat. Spread vegetables in a single layer. Roast, uncovered, for 15 to 20 minutes or until vegetables are light brown on the edges, stirring once.

2. In a large Dutch oven combine roasted vegetables, the water, pork hocks, split peas, savory, and ¼ teaspoon pepper. Bring to boiling; reduce heat. Simmer, covered, for 45 minutes, stirring occasionally. Remove pork hocks from Dutch oven; set aside.

3. Stir frozen peas and parsley into soup in Dutch oven; cool slightly. Using a handheld immersion blender, blend soup leaving some chunky pieces. (Or transfer soup, half at a time, to a food processor or blender. Cover and process or blend leaving some chunky pieces.) Return puree to Dutch oven. Stir in lemon juice.

4. When pork hocks are cool enough to handle, remove meat from bones, discarding bones. Coarsely shred enough of the meat to measure ¾ cup; set aside. Chop the remaining meat. Stir the chopped meat into puree. (To serve today, continue cooking as directed in Steps 6 and 7.)

5. Transfer soup and the reserved shredded meat to separate freezer containers. Cover and freeze up to 2 months.

6. To serve, thaw soup and the reserved shredded meat in the refrigerator for 1 to 2 days. Transfer thawed or chilled soup to a large Dutch oven. Cook over medium heat about 25 minutes or until heated through, stirring occasionally.

7. Season to taste with salt and pepper. Sprinkle servings with reserved shredded meat.

Per serving: 267 cal., 5 g fat (1 g sat. fat), 25 mg chol., 663 mg sodium, 35 g carb., 13 g fiber, 21 g pro.

To refrigerate rather than freeze soup, follow directions through Step 4. Transfer soup and the reserved shredded meat to separate airtight containers. Cover and refrigerate up to 3 days. To serve, continue as directed in Steps 6 and 7.

▶▶▶ pumpkin, barley, and andouille soup

MAKE AHEAD UP TO 2 MONTHS

PREP: 30 minutes   FREEZE: up to 2 months   THAW: 1 to 2 days
HEAT: 25 minutes   MAKES: 4 servings

- 1 tablespoon vegetable oil
- 8 ounces cooked andouille or smoked sausage links, chopped
- ⅓ cup chopped onion (1 small)
- 4 cups water
- 1 cup quick-cooking barley
- 1 tablespoon snipped fresh sage or 1 teaspoon dried sage, crushed
- 1 teaspoon instant chicken bouillon granules
- 1 15-ounce can pumpkin
- 2 tablespoons maple syrup
- 1 tablespoon cider vinegar
  - Salt
  - Black pepper
  - Fresh sage leaves (optional)

1. In a 4-quart Dutch oven heat oil over medium heat. Add sausage and onion; cook for 3 minutes, stirring frequently. Add the water, barley, dried sage (if using), and bouillon granules.

2. Bring to boiling; reduce heat. Simmer, covered, for 12 minutes, stirring occasionally. Stir in pumpkin, maple syrup, and vinegar. (To serve today, cook until heated through as directed in Step 4, and continue through Step 5.)

3. Cool soup slightly and transfer to freezer containers. Cover and freeze for up to 2 months.

4. To serve, thaw soup in the refrigerator for 1 to 2 days. Transfer thawed or chilled soup to a 4-quart Dutch oven. Cook over medium heat about 25 minutes or until heated through, stirring occasionally.

5. If using, stir in snipped fresh sage. Season to taste with salt and pepper. If desired, sprinkle each serving with fresh sage leaves.

Per serving: *439 cal., 21 g fat (6 g sat. fat), 35 mg chol., 832 mg sodium, 51 g carb., 11 g fiber, 14 g pro.*

TIP

To refrigerate rather than freeze soup, follow directions through Step 2. Cool soup slightly then transfer to an airtight container. Cover and refrigerate up to 3 days. To serve, follow directions in Steps 4 and 5.

▶▶▶ chicken-verde tamales

MAKE AHEAD UP TO 6 MONTHS

PREP: 1½ hours   STAND: 30 minutes   FREEZE: up to 6 months
COOK: 45 minutes   MAKES: 12 servings

1 tablespoon vegetable oil	36 dried cornhusks (each about 8 inches long and 6 inches wide at narrow end)
¾ cup chopped red sweet pepper (1 medium)	Boiling water
½ cup chopped onion (1 medium)	1 cup lard or shortening
2 cloves garlic, minced	2 teaspoons baking powder
2½ cups shredded cooked chicken	4 cups masa harina (corn tortilla flour)
1 cup crumbled queso fresco or shredded Monterey Jack cheese	1 teaspoon salt
⅔ cup salsa verde (green salsa)	2 cups chicken broth

1. For the filling, in a large skillet heat oil over medium-low heat. Add sweet pepper, onion, and garlic. Cook about 5 minutes or until vegetables are softened, stirring occasionally. Add chicken, queso fresco, and salsa verde; cook about 2 minutes or until heated through. Set aside until needed.

2. In a large bowl combine cornhusks and enough boiling water to cover. Weight down with a heavy pan lid or plate. Let stand about 30 minutes or until husks are soft and pliable. Drain well; pat dry with paper towels.

3. Meanwhile, for dough, in a large mixing bowl beat lard and baking powder with an electric mixer on medium speed about 2 minutes or until smooth. In a medium bowl stir together masa harina and salt. Alternately add masa harina mixture and broth to lard mixture, beating until dough resembles a thick, creamy paste.

4. To assemble each tamale, start about 1 inch from the narrow end of a cornhusk and spread about 2 tablespoons of the dough into a 4×3-inch rectangle, one long side of the dough is at a long edge of the husk. Spoon 1 rounded tablespoon of the filling along the center of dough. Fold long edge of husk over filling so it overlaps dough slightly. Roll husk around outside of filled dough. Tie ends with strips of cornhusk or 100-percent-cotton kitchen string. (To serve today, continue as directed in Step 6, beginning with pouring water in Dutch oven.)

5. To freeze tamales, place tamales in a resealable freezer bag or a freezer container. Seal and freeze up to 6 months.

6. To serve, do not thaw tamales. Pour enough water into the bottom of an extra-large Dutch oven to reach a depth of 1½ inches. Bring to boiling. Stand tamales upright in a steamer basket (if desired, place a cone-shape ball of foil in the center of the basket). Fill the space in the steamer basket, without packing tamales tightly. Carefully place basket in Dutch oven over boiling water. Reduce heat to medium-low. Cover and steam for 45 to 60 minutes or until dough easily pulls away from cornhusks and is spongy and cooked through.

Per serving: 413 cal., 25 g fat (9 g sat. fat), 51 mg chol., 609 mg sodium, 35 g carb., 5 g fiber, 15 g pro.

▶▶▶ chicken-andouille lasagna

MAKE AHEAD UP TO 1 MONTH

PREP: 45 minutes   FREEZE: up to 1 month   THAW: 12 hours
BAKE: 1 hour + 10 minutes at 350°F   STAND: 15 minutes   MAKES: 12 servings

- 16 dried lasagna noodles
- 1 pound cooked andouille sausage or smoked pork sausage links, quartered lengthwise and sliced
- 1 pound skinless, boneless chicken breast halves, cut into ¾-inch pieces
- 2 to 3 teaspoons Cajun seasoning
- 1 teaspoon dried sage, crushed
- ½ cup chopped onion (1 medium)
- ½ cup chopped celery (1 stalk)
- ½ cup chopped red and/or green sweet pepper
- 6 cloves garlic, minced
- 2 10-ounce containers refrigerated Alfredo pasta sauce
- ½ cup grated Parmesan cheese
- Nonstick cooking spray
- 1½ cups shredded mozzarella cheese (6 ounces)
- Grated Parmesan cheese (optional)
- Snipped fresh Italian (flat-leaf) parsley (optional)

1. Cook lasagna noodles according to package directions; drain. Rinse with cold water; drain again.

2. Meanwhile, in a large skillet combine sausage, chicken, Cajun seasoning, and sage. Cook for 8 minutes or until meat is no longer pink, stirring frequently. Using a slotted spoon, remove meat mixture, reserving drippings in skillet. Set meat mixture aside. Add onion, celery, sweet pepper, and garlic to the reserved drippings; cook until vegetables are tender, stirring occasionally. Return meat mixture to skillet. Stir in half the Alfredo sauce and the ½ cup Parmesan cheese.

3. To assemble lasagna, lightly coat a 3-quart rectangular baking dish with cooking spray. Place four noodles in the prepared baking dish, cutting as necessary to fit bottom of the dish. Spread with one-third of the meat mixture; sprinkle with one-third of the mozzarella cheese. Repeat layers twice. Top with the remaining four noodles. Carefully spread the remaining Alfredo sauce over the top. Cover baking dish with foil. (To serve today, continue as directed in Step 4, beginning with preheating oven. To freeze, wrap dish for up to 1 month.)

4. To serve, thaw frozen lasagna in the refrigerator overnight. Lasagna may still be a bit icy. Preheat oven to 350°F. Bake, covered, for 1 hour. Bake, uncovered, for 10 to 15 minutes more or until heated through. Let stand for 15 to 20 minutes before serving. If desired, sprinkle with additional Parmesan cheese and parsley.

Per serving: 433 cal., 25 g fat (13 g sat. fat), 81 mg chol., 922 mg sodium, 28 g carb., 1 g fiber, 24 g pro.

For long-term storage of individual portions, assemble and bake the lasagna. Cool completely. Cut into individual servings; wrap each portion in plastic wrap, then in aluminum foil. Freeze up to 1 month.

▶▶▶ ravioli lasagna with chianti sauce

MAKE AHEAD UP TO 1 MONTH

PREP: 45 minutes   FREEZE: up to 1 month   THAW: 12 hours   BAKE: 1 hour 15 minutes at 375°F
STAND: 10 minutes   MAKES: 8 servings

- 2 tablespoons olive oil
- ½ cup chopped onion (1 medium)
- 3 cloves garlic, minced
- 1 28-ounce can crushed tomatoes
- 1 cup Chianti or other full-flavor dry red wine
- 2 teaspoons dried Italian seasoning, crushed
- ¼ to ½ teaspoon crushed red pepper
- 12 ounces Italian-flavor cooked chicken sausage links, halved lengthwise and sliced ½ inch thick
- 4½ cups sliced fresh cremini or button mushrooms (12 ounces)
- 1 7-ounce jar roasted red sweet peppers, drained and coarsely chopped
- ½ cup snipped fresh basil
- 2 9-ounce packages refrigerated cheese-filled ravioli
- 2 cups shredded mozzarella cheese (8 ounces)

1. For sauce, in a large saucepan heat 1 tablespoon of the oil over medium heat. Add onion and garlic; cook about 3 minutes or until onion is tender, stirring occasionally. Stir in tomatoes, Chianti, Italian seasoning, and crushed red pepper. Bring to boiling; reduce heat. Simmer, uncovered, about 10 minutes or until sauce is slightly thickened.

2. Meanwhile, for the sausage layer, in an extra-large skillet heat the remaining 1 tablespoon oil over medium heat. Add sausage and mushrooms; cook until mushrooms are tender, stirring occasionally. Stir in roasted peppers and basil.

3. To assemble lasagna, spread one-fourth of the sauce in an ungreased 3-quart rectangular baking dish. Layer with one package of the ravioli and half the sausage mixture. Spread another one-fourth of the sauce over sausage layer in dish. Sprinkle with half the cheese; spread another one-fourth of the sauce over cheese in dish. Top with the remaining ravioli, sausage mixture, sauce, and cheese. (To serve today, continue with Step 5. Bake, covered, for 35 minutes. Bake, uncovered, for 5 minutes more or until heated through and cheese is bubbly.)

4. To freeze lasagna, cover baking dish with plastic wrap, then with foil. Freeze up to 1 month.

5. To serve, thaw frozen lasagna in the refrigerator overnight (lasagna may still be a bit icy). Preheat oven to 375°F. Remove plastic wrap; cover with foil. Bake for 1 hour. Bake, uncovered, about 15 minutes more or until lasagna is heated through and cheese is bubbly. Let stand for 10 minutes before serving.

Per serving: *445 cal., 18 g fat (8 g sat. fat), 87 mg chol., 993 mg sodium, 42 g carb., 5 g fiber, 27 g pro.*

Avoid using aluminum foil to wrap dishes that contain acidic foods, such as tomatoes. Acid reacts with foil, which can give foods an off flavor. If you would like to use foil, wrap the lasagna in plastic wrap first.

▶▶▶ chicken, wild rice, and vegetable casserole

MAKE AHEAD UP TO 2 MONTHS

PREP: 25 minutes   FREEZE: up to 2 months   THAW: 1 to 2 days
BAKE: 1 hour at 350°F   MAKES: 8 servings

- 1 6-ounce package long grain and wild rice mix
- 3 cups chopped cooked chicken
- 2 cups frozen French-cut green beans, thawed
- 1 10.75-ounce can condensed cream of celery soup
- 1 8-ounce can sliced water chestnuts, drained
- ½ cup mayonnaise or salad dressing
- ½ cup chopped onion (1 medium)
- 3 tablespoons sliced almonds
- 1 2-ounce jar sliced pimientos, drained
- 1 tablespoon lemon juice
- 1 cup shredded cheddar cheese (4 ounces)

1. Cook rice mix according to package directions.

2. Meanwhile, in an extra-large bowl combine chicken, green beans, cream of celery soup, water chestnuts, mayonnaise, onion, almonds, pimientos, and lemon juice. Add cooked rice mix to chicken mixture; stir to combine. Spoon into a 3-quart rectangular baking dish. (To serve today, proceed with Step 4, beginning with preheating the oven. Bake, covered, for 30 minutes.)

3. To freeze the casserole, cover baking dish with plastic wrap, then foil. Freeze up to 2 months.

4. To serve, thaw frozen casserole in the refrigerator for 1 to 2 days or until completely thawed before baking. Preheat oven to 350°F. Remove plastic wrap. Cover with foil. Bake thawed casserole for 55 minutes. Sprinkle with cheese. Bake, uncovered, about 5 minutes more or until heated through and cheese is melted.

Per serving: 422 cal., 24 g fat (7 g sat. fat), 68 mg chol., 773 mg sodium, 30 g carb., 3 g fiber, 23 g pro.

To refrigerate rather than freeze the casserole, follow directions through Step 2. Cover baking dish with plastic wrap, then with foil. Refrigerate up to 24 hours. To serve, continue as directed in Step 4, except bake, covered, for 45 minutes.

▶▶▶ parmesan chicken and broccoli

MAKE AHEAD UP TO 3 MONTHS

PREP: 30 minutes   FREEZE: up to 3 months   THAW: 1 or 2 days
BAKE: 1 hour at 350°F   MAKES: 4 servings per casserole

        2 cups uncooked converted rice
        1 cup chopped onion (1 large)
        2 tablespoons butter
    2½ teaspoons dried Italian seasoning, crushed
        2 tablespoons vegetable oil
        2 pounds skinless, boneless chicken breast halves, cut into bite-size strips
        3 cloves garlic, minced
        1 24-ounce package frozen cut broccoli (6 cups)
        2 10.75-ounce cans condensed cream of mushroom soup or cream of chicken soup
        1 cup water
        1 cup chopped tomato (1 large)
      ⅔ cup grated Parmesan cheese
        Salt
        Black pepper

1. Cook rice according to package directions; remove from heat. Stir in half of the onion, the butter, and 1 teaspoon of the Italian seasoning. Divide the rice mixture among three 2-quart baking dishes or casseroles; set aside.

2. In an extra-large skillet heat oil over medium heat. Add the remaining onion, the remaining Italian seasoning, the chicken, and garlic; cook and stir for 4 to 6 minutes or until chicken is no longer pink. Remove from heat. Stir in frozen broccoli, soup, the water, tomato, and Parmesan cheese. Season to taste with salt and pepper.

3. Spoon chicken mixture over rice in dishes. Cover baking dishes with foil. Freeze up to 3 months.

4. To serve, thaw one baking dish in the refrigerator for 1 to 2 days (casserole may still be icy). Preheat oven to 350°F. Bake, covered, for 30 minutes. Uncover and bake for 30 minutes more or until heated through.

Per serving: *320 cal., 10 g fat (3 g sat. fat), 53 mg chol., 668 mg sodium, 34 g carb., 2 g fiber, 25 g pro.*

For casseroles and stir-fries, cut poultry and meat into bite-size pieces when you get home from the supermarket, then wrap and freeze them. Because the pieces are small, they thaw quickly and are ready to use in no time.

▶▶▶ white chicken chili

MAKE AHEAD UP TO 2 MONTHS

PREP: 40 minutes   COOK: 20 minutes   FREEZE: up to 2 months
THAW: 1 to 2 days   HEAT: 25 minutes   MAKES: 5 servings

1 tablespoon vegetable oil
¾ cup chopped red sweet pepper (1 medium)
½ cup chopped onion (1 medium)
2 cloves garlic, minced
1 pound skinless, boneless chicken thighs, cut into 1-inch pieces
2 14.5-ounce cans reduced-sodium chicken broth
1 19-ounce can cannellini beans (white kidney beans), rinsed and drained
1 12-ounce package frozen white whole kernel corn (shoe peg)

1 4-ounce can diced green chile peppers, undrained
1 teaspoon ground cumin
½ teaspoon salt
½ teaspoon dried oregano, crushed
¼ teaspoon black pepper
½ teaspoon finely shredded lime peel
1 tablespoon lime juice
¼ cup vegetable oil
Salt and black pepper
2 6-inch corn tortillas, cut into narrow strips

1. In a Dutch oven heat 1 tablespoon oil over medium heat. Add sweet pepper, onion, and garlic; cook about 5 minutes or until tender, stirring occasionally. Add chicken; cook and stir for 5 to 7 minutes or until chicken is no longer pink.

2. Stir in broth, beans, corn, chile peppers, cumin, ½ teaspoon salt, oregano, and ¼ teaspoon black pepper. Bring to boiling; reduce heat. Simmer, uncovered, for 20 minutes. Stir in lime peel and lime juice. Using a potato masher, coarsely mash beans. (To serve today, continue as directed in Step 4, beginning with cooking 25 minutes and proceeding through Step 6.)

3. To freeze chili, cool slightly and transfer to freezer containers. Cover and freeze up to 2 months.

4. To serve, thaw frozen chili in the refrigerator for 1 to 2 days. Transfer thawed or chilled chili to a Dutch oven. Cook over medium heat for 25 minutes or until heated through, stirring occasionally.

5. Meanwhile, in a large skillet heat ¼ cup oil over medium heat. Add tortilla strips, half at a time, and cook for 2 minutes or until browned. Remove with a slotted spoon; drain on paper towels.

6. Season chili to taste with additional salt and black pepper. Top each serving with tortilla strips.

Per serving: 430 cal., 19 g fat (2 g sat. fat), 75 mg chol., 1,003 mg sodium, 45 g carb., 11 g fiber, 32 g pro.

TIP

To refrigerate rather than freeze the chili, follow directions through Step 2. Cool chili slightly and transfer to airtight containers. Cover and refrigerate up to 3 days. To serve, continue as directed in Steps 4, 5, and 6.

▶▶▶ chicken in creamy wine and mushroom sauce

MAKE AHEAD UP TO 1 MONTH

PREP: 25 minutes   FREEZE: up to 1 month   THAW: 30 minutes
BAKE: 1 hour 25 minutes at 350°F   MAKES: 6 servings

- 6 skinless, boneless chicken breast halves (about 2 pounds)
- 1 8-ounce package fresh cremini mushrooms, sliced
- 1 10¾-ounce can condensed golden mushroom soup
- ½ cup dry white wine or chicken broth
- ½ of an 8-ounce tub cream cheese spread with chives and onion
- ¼ cup butter, melted
- 3 cloves garlic, minced
- 1 0.7-ounce envelope Italian dry salad dressing mix
- Hot cooked rice or angel hair pasta

1. Place chicken breasts in a single layer in a 3-quart rectangular baking dish. Sprinkle mushrooms on chicken breasts. In a medium bowl whisk together mushroom soup, white wine, cream cheese, butter, garlic, and salad dressing mix until combined; pour over chicken.

2. Cover baking dish with plastic wrap, then foil. Freeze up to 1 month.

3. To serve, let casserole stand at room temperature for 30 minutes to thaw. Preheat oven to 350°F. Remove plastic wrap; cover with foil. Bake for 1¼ hours or until chicken is no longer pink. Remove foil; bake for 10 minutes more. Remove chicken from baking dish and place on a serving platter. Whisk sauce and spoon over chicken. Serve with hot cooked rice or pasta.

Per serving: 442 cal., 19 g fat (10 g sat. fat), 135 mg chol., 1,019 mg sodium, 24 g carb., 1 g fiber, 36 g pro.

Make your own IQF (individually quick frozen) ingredients. To keep chopped vegetables or meats from forming a clump, spread them out on a baking sheet and freeze 1 hour or until firm before packing in a freezer bag.

▶▶▶ gingered chicken meatball soup with brown rice and basil

MAKE AHEAD UP TO 2 MONTHS

PREP: 45 minutes   FREEZE: up to 2 months   THAW: 1 to 2 days
HEAT: 25 minutes   MAKES: 4 servings

2 teaspoons canola oil
¼ cup finely chopped green onions (2)
8 cloves garlic, minced
1 tablespoon grated fresh ginger
2 egg whites
¾ cup panko bread crumbs
½ cup finely chopped red sweet pepper (1 small)
3 tablespoons reduced-sodium soy sauce
2 teaspoons sesame oil

1 pound uncooked ground chicken breast or turkey breast
½ cup chopped sweet onion (1 medium)
2½ cups reduced-sodium chicken broth
1½ cups water
2 tablespoons rice wine vinegar
1 tablespoon honey
1 teaspoon crushed red pepper
1½ cups cooked brown rice
½ cup snipped fresh basil
Asian chili sauce (Sriracha sauce) (optional)

1. In a large nonstick skillet heat canola oil over medium heat. Add green onions; cook and stir about 2 minutes or until tender. Add half the garlic and the ginger; cook and stir for 30 seconds. Remove from heat.

2. In a large bowl combine green onion mixture, egg whites, panko, sweet pepper, 1 tablespoon of the soy sauce, and 1 teaspoon of the sesame oil. Add ground chicken; mix well. Shape chicken mixture into 1-inch meatballs. In the same skillet cook meatballs over medium-high heat until browned, turning occasionally. Set aside.

3. In a large saucepan heat the remaining 1 teaspoon sesame oil over medium-high heat. Add sweet onion; cook for 2 to 3 minutes or until nearly tender, stirring occasionally. Add the remaining garlic; cook and stir for 30 seconds. Add the remaining 2 tablespoons soy sauce, the broth, the water, vinegar, honey, and crushed red pepper. Bring to boiling; stir in meatballs. Return to boiling; reduce heat. Simmer, uncovered, until meatballs are cooked through (165°F). (To serve today, continue as directed in Step 5 beginning with cooking over medium heat and proceeding through Step 6.)

4. To freeze meatball soup, cool slightly then transfer to freezer containers. Cover and freeze up to 2 months.

5. To serve, thaw soup in the refrigerator for 1 to 2 days. Transfer thawed soup to a large saucepan. Cook over medium heat for 25 minutes or until heated through, stirring occasionally.

6. Stir in cooked rice and basil. If desired, serve with Asian chili sauce.

Per serving: *391 cal., 15 g fat (3 g sat. fat), 98 mg chol., 939 mg sodium, 36 g carb., 3 g fiber, 28 g pro.*

▶▶▶chicken-spinach calzones

MAKE AHEAD UP TO 3 MONTHS

PREP: 40 minutes   BAKE: 20 minutes at 375°F/12 minutes at 350°F   COOL: 30 minutes
FREEZE: up to 3 months   THAW: 12 hours   MAKES: 12 servings

Nonstick cooking spray
1 pound cooked chicken breast or turkey breast, chopped (about 3 cups)
2½ cups coarsely chopped fresh spinach
1½ cups shredded part-skim mozzarella cheese (6 ounces)
½ cup no-salt-added tomato sauce or regular tomato sauce
1 teaspoon dried Italian seasoning, crushed
1 clove garlic, minced
2 13.8-ounce packages refrigerated pizza dough
Fat-free milk
Grated Parmesan or Romano cheese (optional)
Pizza sauce, warmed (optional)

1. Preheat oven to 375°F. Lightly coat two large baking sheets with cooking spray; set aside. For filling, in a large bowl combine chicken, spinach, mozzarella cheese, tomato sauce, Italian seasoning, and garlic. On a lightly floured surface, roll out one package of the pizza dough to a 15×10-inch rectangle. Cut rectangle in half lengthwise, then in thirds crosswise to make six 5-inch squares.

2. Place about ⅓ cup filling on half of each square, spreading to within ½ inch of edges. Moisten edges of dough with water then fold over filling, forming a triangle or rectangle. Pinch or press with a fork to seal edges. Prick tops of calzones with a fork; brush with milk. Place on a prepared baking sheet. Repeat with remaining dough and filling.

3. If desired, sprinkle calzones with Parmesan cheese. Bake for 20 minutes or until golden. Transfer to wire racks; cool for 30 minutes.

4. Transfer calzones to an ungreased baking sheet. Cover loosely with plastic wrap; freeze until firm. Transfer to freezer containers. Cover and freeze up to 3 months.

5. To serve, thaw desired number of calzones in the refrigerator overnight. Preheat oven to 350°F. Lightly grease a baking sheet. Arrange calzones on the prepared baking sheet. Bake calzones for 12 to 15 minutes or until heated through. If desired, serve with warmed pizza sauce.

Per serving: *270 cal., 6 g fat (2 g sat. fat), 41 mg chol., 483 mg sodium, 32 g carb., 1 g fiber, 21 g pro.*

Calzones are an ideal make-ahead meal when everyone is on a different schedule. Thaw and heat just the number needed—and leave the rest in the freezer for another time.

▶▶▶ cheesy tuna noodle casserole

MAKE AHEAD UP TO 1 MONTH

PREP: 30 minutes   FREEZE: up to 1 month   THAW: 12 hours   BAKE: 1 hour 5 minutes at 375°F
MAKES: 6 servings

- 3 cups dried wide egg noodles
- ¼ cup butter
- 1 cup chopped red sweet pepper
- 1 cup chopped celery (2 stalks)
- ¼ cup chopped onion
- ¼ cup all-purpose flour
- 1 to 2 tablespoons Dijon-style mustard
- ½ teaspoon salt
- ¼ teaspoon black pepper
- 2¼ cups milk
- 1 12-ounce can chunk white tuna (water pack), drained and broken into chunks, or two 5-ounce pouches chunk light tuna in water, drained
- 1 cup cubed cheddar cheese
- ½ cup panko bread crumbs or soft bread crumbs
- ¼ cup freshly grated Parmesan cheese (1 ounce)
- 1 tablespoon snipped fresh Italian (flat-leaf) parsley
- 1 tablespoon butter, melted

1. Lightly grease a 2-quart rectangular baking dish; set aside. In a large saucepan cook noodles according to package directions; drain. Return noodles to pan.

2. Meanwhile, for sauce, in a medium saucepan melt ¼ cup butter over medium heat. Add sweet pepper, celery, and onion; cook for 8 to 10 minutes or until tender, stirring occasionally. Stir in flour, mustard, salt, and black pepper. Gradually stir in milk. Cook and stir until slightly thickened and bubbly.

3. Gently fold sauce, tuna, and cheddar cheese into cooked noodles. Transfer noodle mixture to the prepared baking dish. For topping, in a small bowl stir together panko, Parmesan cheese, and parsley; stir in melted butter. Sprinkle over casserole. (To serve today, continue as directed in Step 5, beginning with preheating the oven. Bake, uncovered, for 25 to 30 minutes.)

4. To freeze casserole, cover baking dish with plastic wrap, then with foil. Freeze up to 1 month.

5. To serve, thaw frozen casserole in the refrigerator overnight (casserole may still be a bit icy). Preheat oven to 375°F. Bake, uncovered, for 65 to 75 minutes or until heated through. Let stand for 5 minutes before serving.

Per serving: *416 cal., 22 g fat (13 g sat. fat), 95 mg chol., 779 mg sodium, 28 g carb., 2 g fiber, 25 g pro.*

When reheating leftovers or any food that has been refrigerated or frozen, be sure it is heated to a safe internal temperature before serving. Heat casseroles to 165°F. Bring sauces, soups, and gravies to a full boil.

▶▶▶ manhattan clam chowder

MAKE AHEAD UP TO 2 MONTHS

PREP: 40 minutes   FREEZE: up to 2 months   THAW: 1 to 2 days
HEAT: 25 minutes   MAKES: 4 servings

- 6 6.5-ounce cans minced clams
- 1 cup chopped celery (2 stalks)
- ⅓ cup chopped onion (1 small)
- ¼ cup chopped carrot
- 2 tablespoons olive oil or vegetable oil
- 2 cups reduced-sodium chicken broth
- 1 8-ounce bottle clam juice or 1 cup chicken broth
- 2 cups cubed red-skinned potatoes (2 medium)
- ¼ cup tomato paste
- 1 teaspoon dried thyme, crushed
- ⅛ teaspoon cayenne pepper
- ⅛ teaspoon black pepper
- 1 14.5-ounce can diced tomatoes, undrained
- ¼ cup broken, crisp-cooked bacon or purchased cooked bacon pieces (see tip, below)

1. Drain clams, discarding juice or reserving for another use. Set clams aside.

2. In a large saucepan cook celery, onion, and carrot in hot oil over medium heat until tender, stirring occasionally. Stir in 2 cups broth and bottled clam juice. Stir in potatoes, tomato paste, thyme, cayenne pepper, and black pepper. Bring to boiling; reduce heat. Simmer, covered, for 10 to 12 minutes or until potatoes are tender. Stir in clams and tomatoes. (To serve today, top each serving with bacon.)

3. To freeze chowder, cool slightly then transfer to freezer containers. Seal and freeze up to 2 months.

4. To serve, thaw chowder in the refrigerator for 1 to 2 days. Transfer thawed soup to a large saucepan. Cook over medium heat for 25 minutes or until heated through, stirring occasionally. Top each serving with bacon.

Per serving: 409 cal., 13 g fat (3 g sat. fat), 78 mg chol., 1,088 mg sodium, 32 g carb., 5 g fiber, 42 g pro.

If you prefer to cook the bacon, cook four slices, reserving
2 tablespoons of the drippings. Cook the celery, onion, and carrot in the
reserved drippings, omitting the cooking oil.

▶▶▶ vegetarian chili

MAKE AHEAD UP TO 2 MONTHS

PREP: 40 minutes   FREEZE: up to 2 months   THAW: 1 to 2 days
HEAT: 30 minutes   MAKES: 8 servings

- 1 cup chopped red, green, and/or yellow sweet peppers (2 small)
- ½ cup chopped onion (1 medium)
- 3 cloves garlic, minced
- 1 tablespoon vegetable oil
- 4 14.5-ounce cans diced tomatoes with chili spices or diced tomatoes, undrained
- 1 12-ounce can beer or one 14.5-ounce can vegetable broth
- 1 cup water
- 1 8-ounce can tomato sauce
- 3 to 4 teaspoons chili powder
- 1 tablespoon snipped fresh oregano or 1 teaspoon dried oregano, crushed
- 1 teaspoon ground cumin

- ½ teaspoon black pepper
  Several dashes bottled hot pepper sauce (optional)
- 3 15-ounce cans pinto beans, black beans, cannellini beans (white kidney beans), and/or red kidney beans, rinsed and drained
- 2 cups fresh or frozen whole kernel corn
- 1 cup chopped zucchini and/or yellow summer squash (1 small)
- 1 cup shredded cheddar cheese or Monterey Jack cheese (4 ounces) (optional)
  Coarsely chopped peeled avocado (optional)
  Fresh oregano sprigs (optional)

1. In a 5- to 6-quart Dutch oven cook sweet peppers, onion, and garlic in hot oil over medium heat until tender, stirring occasionally. Stir in tomatoes, beer, the water, tomato sauce, chili powder, dried oregano (if using), cumin, black pepper, and, if desired, hot pepper sauce. Bring to boiling; reduce heat. Simmer, covered, for 10 minutes.

2. Stir in beans, corn, and zucchini. Return to boiling; reduce heat. Simmer, uncovered, for 10 minutes. (To serve today, continue with Step 5.)

3. To freeze chili, cool slightly and transfer to freezer containers. Cover and freeze up to 2 months.

4. To serve, thaw chili in the refrigerator for 1 to 2 days. Transfer thawed or refrigerated chili to a 5- to 6-quart Dutch oven. Cook over medium heat for 30 minutes or until heated through, stirring occasionally.

5. If using, stir in the 1 tablespoon snipped fresh oregano. If desired, sprinkle servings with cheese, avocado, and fresh oregano sprigs.

Per serving: 276 cal., 5 g fat (1 g sat. fat), 0 mg chol., 1,268 mg sodium, 46 g carb., 11 g fiber, 12 g pro.

To refrigerate rather than freeze the chili, cool it slightly then transfer it to airtight containers. Cover and refrigerate for up to 3 days. Continue as directed in Steps 4 and 5.

▶▶▶ spinach-three cheese-stuffed pasta shells

MAKE AHEAD UP TO 1 MONTH

PREP: 30 minutes   FREEZE: up to 1 month   THAW: 30 minutes
BAKE: 1 hour 45 minutes at 350°F   MAKES: 4 servings

    12 dried jumbo shell pasta
     1 10-ounce package frozen chopped spinach, thawed
     2 eggs
     1 8-ounce package shredded mozzarella cheese (2 cups)
     1 cup ricotta cheese
    ¼ cup shredded Parmesan cheese
     1 26- to 32-ounce jar pasta sauce

1. Cook pasta according to package directions; drain. Rinse with cold water; drain again. Meanwhile, drain thawed spinach well, pressing out excess liquid.

2. For filling, in a medium bowl beat eggs. Stir in spinach, 1½ cups of the mozzarella cheese, the ricotta cheese, and Parmesan cheese. Spoon 2 rounded tablespoons of the filling into each jumbo shell. Spread about ½ cup of the pasta sauce on the bottom of a 2-quart square baking dish. Place shells in dish. Pour pasta sauce over shells. Sprinkle with remaining ½ cup mozzarella cheese.

3. Cover with plastic wrap, then with foil. Freeze up to 1 month.

4. To serve, thaw casserole at room temperature for 30 minutes. Preheat oven to 350°F. Remove plastic wrap; cover with foil. Bake for 1½ hours. Remove foil. Bake 15 minutes more or until heated through (165°F).

Per serving: *508 cal., 24 g fat (13 g sat. fat), 168 mg chol., 1,347 mg sodium, 39 g carb., 6 g fiber, 34 g pro.*

To avoid leaving a baking dish in the freezer for weeks, line it with plastic wrap. Fill the prepared dish with casserole ingredients, wrap the dish and freeze overnight (or several hours). When frozen, lift out the food and place in a freezer bag; freeze up to 1 month. To thaw, remove plastic wrap and return food to the original baking dish. Thaw and bake as directed.

▶▶▶ pepper and basil tortellini soup

MAKE AHEAD UP TO 1 MONTH

PREP: 20 minutes   FREEZE: Up to 1 month   COOK: 20 minutes   MAKES: 4 servings

    1 14.5-ounce can Italian-style stewed tomatoes, undrained
 1¼ cups water
    1 9-ounce package refrigerated three cheese-filled tortellini
    1 cup chopped red and/or yellow sweet peppers
  ⅓ cup snipped fresh basil
    1 14.5-ounce can reduced-sodium vegetable or chicken broth
        Salt
        Grated Parmesan cheese (optional)

1. In a 1-gallon freezer bag combine tomatoes, the water, tortellini, sweet peppers, and basil. Squeeze air from bag, seal, and freeze for up to 1 month.

2. To serve, in a large saucepan bring broth to boiling; add frozen ingredients. Return to boiling; reduce heat. Simmer, covered, about 20 minutes or until heated through, stirring occasionally. Season to taste with salt. If desired, top each serving with Parmesan cheese.

Per serving : 241 cal., 4 g total fat (2 g sat. fat), 24 mg chol., 828 mg sodium, 39 g carb., 4 g fiber, 8 g sugar, 12 g pro.

To serve this soup today, place all of the ingredients—except for the salt and Parmesan cheese—in a large saucepan and cook until heated through.

▶▶▶ portobello soup

MAKE AHEAD UP TO 1 MONTH

PREP: 30 minutes   FREEZE: Up to 1 month   COOK: 3 minutes   MAKES: 6 servings

6 cups fresh portobello mushrooms (16 ounces)
1 tablespoon olive oil
2 cloves garlic, minced
1 teaspoon dried thyme, crushed
¼ teaspoon crushed red pepper
3 cups fresh baby spinach
1 8.8-ounce pouch cooked long grain and wild rice
8 ounces zucchini, cut into 1- to 1½-inch pieces
8 ounces yellow summer squash, cut into 1- to 1½-inch pieces
3 14.5-ounce cans low sodium vegetable broth or 50% less sodium beef broth
1 tablespoon balsamic vinegar
¼ teaspoon salt
¼ teaspoon black pepper
  Shaved Pamesan cheese (optional)

1. Remove stems and gills from mushrooms. Slice mushroom caps; cut slices crosswise into 2-inch pieces.

2. In a very large skillet heat oil over medium-high heat. Add mushroom pieces, garlic, thyme, and crushed red pepper; cook about 6 minutes or until mushrooms are browned, stirring occasionally. (To serve today, add spinach, rice, zucchini, and yellow squash and continue with Step 4.)

3. Spread mushroom mixture on a sheet of foil to cool quickly. In a 1-gallon freezer bag combine mushroom mixture, spinach, rice, zucchini, and yellow squash. Squeeze air from bag, seal, and freeze for up to 1 month.

4. To serve, in a large saucepan bring broth, vinegar, salt, and black pepper to boiling; add frozen ingredients. Return to boiling; reduce heat. Simmer about 3 minutes or until soup is heated through and vegetables are tender, stirring occasionally. If desired, top each serving with cheese.

Per serving: 133 cal., 4 g total fat (0 g sat. fat), 0 mg chol., 717 mg sodium, 20 g carb., 3 g fiber, 5 g sugar, 6 g pro.

slow cooker ▶
RECIPES

By definition, using a slow cooker is making a meal ahead—hours ahead—of when you want to eat it. These recipes go one step further. Prep and seal them in a slow cooker liner the night before—then just drop the liner in the cooker the next morning, flip the switch to "on," and head out.

recipes ▸ HOURS AHEAD

▶ texas beef with butternut squash

MAKE AHEAD UP TO 12 HOURS

PREP: 25 minutes   CHILL: up to 12 hours
COOK: 8 to 10 hours (low) or 4 to 5 hours (high)   MAKES: 8 servings

- 1½ **pounds beef chuck roast**
- 4 **cups 1½-inch cubes peeled butternut squash**
- 2 **14.5-ounce cans fire-roasted diced tomatoes, undrained**
- 1½ **cups no-salt-added beef broth or water**
- ¾ **cup chopped onion**
- 1 **4-ounce can diced green chiles**
- 1 **tablespoon ground ancho chile pepper**
- 2 **teaspoons unsweetened cocoa powder**
- 1 **teaspoon ground cumin**
- 1 **teaspoon dried oregano, crushed**
- 3 **cloves garlic, minced**
- **Snipped fresh cilantro**
- **Hot cooked polenta or hot cooked rice (optional)**

1. Place a disposable slow cooker liner in a 5- to 6-quart ceramic slow cooker. Trim beef roast and cut beef into 2-inch pieces. Place beef, squash, tomatoes, beef broth, onion, chiles, chile pepper, cocoa powder, cumin, oregano, and garlic in disposable liner. Using a twist tie, close the disposable liner. Place the ceramic liner in the refrigerator overnight. (To serve today, cover and cook as directed in Step 2.)

2. Place the ceramic liner in the slow cooker. Remove the twist tie from disposable liner. Cover and cook on low-heat setting for 8 to 10 hours or on high-heat setting for 4 to 5 hours. Sprinkle each serving with cilantro. If desired, serve with polenta or hot cooked rice.

Per serving: 258 cal., 13 g fat (5 g sat. fat), 75 mg chol., 313 mg sodium, 16 g carb., 4 g fiber, 19 g pro.

To save time cutting up the meat, look for precut beef stew meat in the meat department of your supermarket. The pieces may be a little smaller than 2 inches, but it will save you a few minutes of prep time.

▶ brisket ciabatta sandwiches

MAKE AHEAD UP TO 12 HOURS

PREP: 30 minutes   CHILL: up to 12 hours
COOK: 9 to 10 hours (low) or 4½ to 5 hours (high)   MAKES: 12 servings

- 1 3-pound fresh beef brisket
- 1 cup sliced fresh cremini or button mushrooms
- ½ cup chopped onion (1 medium)
- 2 cloves garlic, minced
- 1 14.5-ounce can fire-roasted crushed tomatoes or diced tomatoes, undrained
- ½ of a 6-ounce can (⅓ cup) tomato paste with Italian seasonings or plain tomato paste
- ¼ cup dry red wine or beef broth
- 1½ teaspoons Worcestershire sauce
- 1 teaspoon dried Italian seasoning, crushed
- ½ teaspoon salt
- ¼ teaspoon black pepper
- 12 ciabatta buns, split and, if desired, toasted
  Shredded Italian cheese blend or Parmesan cheese (optional)
  Arugula (optional)

1. Place a disposable slow cooker liner in a 4- to 5-quart ceramic slow cooker liner. Trim fat from meat. If necessary, cut meat to fit slow cooker. Place mushrooms, onion, and garlic in disposable liner. Top with meat.

2. For sauce, in a medium bowl combine tomatoes, tomato paste, wine, Worcestershire sauce, Italian seasoning, salt, and pepper. Pour over meat. Using a twist tie, close the disposable liner. Place the ceramic liner in the refrigerator overnight. (To serve today, cover and cook as directed in Step 3.)

3. Place ceramic liner in the slow cooker. Remove the twist tie from the disposable liner. Cover and cook on low-heat setting for 9 to 10 hours or on high-heat setting for 4½ to 5 hours or until meat is tender. Transfer meat to a cutting board; cover with foil and keep warm. Skim fat from sauce.

4. If sauce is thin, transfer to a medium saucepan. Bring to boiling; reduce heat. Simmer, uncovered, for 5 to 10 minutes or until slightly thickened.

5. Coarsely chop meat. Stir some of the sauce into the meat. Divide meat among bottom halves of buns. Spoon some of the sauce over meat. Top with cheese and arugula, if desired, then bun tops. Pass any remaining sauce.

Per serving: *596 cal., 26 g fat (10 g sat. fat), 81 mg chol., 809 mg sodium, 60 g carb., 3 g fiber, 30 g pro.*

▶ brisket with ale barbecue sauce

MAKE AHEAD UP TO 12 HOURS

PREP: 25 minutes   CHILL: up to 12 hours
COOK: 10 to 12 hours (low) or 5 to 6 hours (high)   MAKES: 10 servings

- 1 3- to 4-pound boneless beef brisket
- 2 medium onions, thinly sliced and separated into rings
- 1 bay leaf
- 1 12-ounce can beer
- ¼ cup chili sauce
- 2 tablespoons packed brown sugar
- 1 clove garlic, minced
- ½ teaspoon dried thyme, crushed
- ¼ teaspoon salt
- ¼ teaspoon black pepper
- 2 tablespoons cornstarch
- 2 tablespoons cold water

1. Place a disposable slow cooker liner in a 3½- or 4-quart ceramic slow cooker liner. Trim fat from meat. If necessary, cut meat to fit into a slow cooker. Place onions and bay leaf in disposable liner; add meat. In a medium bowl combine beer, chili sauce, brown sugar, garlic, thyme, salt, and pepper. Pour over meat. Using a twist tie, close the disposable liner. Place the ceramic liner in the refrigerator overnight. (To serve today, cover and cook as directed in Step 2.)

2. Place ceramic liner in the slow cooker. Remove the twist tie from the disposable liner. Cover and cook on low-heat setting for 10 to 12 hours or high-heat setting for 5 to 6 hours.

3. Using a slotted spoon transfer meat and onions to a serving platter. Slice meat across the grain; cover and keep warm. Discard bay leaf.

4. For ale barbecue sauce, pour enough of the cooking liquid into a 4-cup glass measuring cup to equal 2½ cups; skim off fat. Discard the remaining cooking liquid. In a medium saucepan combine cornstarch and the cold water; stir in the 2½ cups cooking liquid. Cook and stir over medium heat until thickened and bubbly, then cook 2 minutes more. Serve brisket and onions with sauce.

Per serving: *182 cal., 6 g fat (2 g sat. fat), 57 mg chol., 217 mg sodium, 9 g carb., 1 g fiber, 20 g pro.*

Brisket, also sold as flat cut or point cut, is one of the least tender cuts of beef, but long, moist cooking renders it butter-knife tender. The point cut has a bit more fat and flavor than the flat cut, which is quite lean.

▶ pot roast paprikash

MAKE AHEAD UP TO 12 HOURS

PREP: 25 minutes   CHILL: up to 12 hours
COOK: 10 to 12 hours (low) or 5 to 6 hours + 30 minutes (high)   MAKES: 8 servings

- 1 2½-pound beef rump roast
- 2 tablespoons paprika
- ½ teaspoon smoked paprika
- 1 14.5-ounce can diced tomatoes, undrained
- 1 14.5-ounce can beef broth
- 3 medium onions, halved and cut into ½-inch slices
- 3 large carrots, coarsely chopped
- 1 12-ounce jar roasted red sweet peppers, drained and cut into ½-inch-wide strips
- ¼ cup water
- 2 tablespoons cornstarch
- 1 8-ounce carton sour cream
-   Salt
-   Black pepper
- 4 ounces dried medium noodles
- ¼ cup butter
- ⅓ cup snipped fresh Italian (flat-leaf) parsley

1. Place a disposable slow cooker liner in a 4- to 5-quart ceramic slow cooker liner. Trim fat from meat; cut into four pieces and place in disposable liner. In a small bowl combine paprika and smoked paprika; sprinkle on meat. Top with tomatoes, broth, onions, carrots, and sweet peppers. Using a twist tie, close the disposable liner. Place the ceramic liner in the refrigerator overnight. (To serve today, cover and cook as directed in Step 2.)

2. Place ceramic liner in the slow cooker. Remove the twist tie from the disposable liner. Cover and cook on low-heat setting for 10 to 12 hours or on high-heat setting for 5 to 6 hours.

3. Using tongs, transfer meat to a cutting board. Use two forks to pull meat apart into coarse shreds. Skim fat from cooking liquid; add meat. If on low-heat setting turn to high-heat setting. In a small bowl whisk together the water and cornstarch; stir into cooker. Cover and cook for 30 minutes. Stir in sour cream. Season to taste with salt and black pepper.

4. Meanwhile, cook noodles according to package directions; drain. Toss with butter. Serve pot roast paprikash over noodles. Sprinkle with parsley.

Per serving: 523 cal., 28 g fat (13 g sat. fat), 136 mg chol., 590 mg sodium, 35 g carb., 4 g fiber, 34 g pro.

▶ chili-orange short ribs

MAKE AHEAD UP TO 12 HOURS

PREP: 20 minutes   CHILL: up to 12 hours
COOK: 11 to 12 hours (low) or 5½ to 6 hours (high)   MAKES: 6 servings

4 to 5 pounds beef short ribs	1 dried chile de arbol pepper
1½ teaspoons kosher salt	½ cup dry sherry or beef broth
½ teaspoon freshly black pepper	4 2-inch strips orange peel
3 medium leeks, trimmed and cut into 2-inch lengths	½ cup orange juice
6 cloves garlic, sliced	¼ cup reduced-sodium soy sauce
1 1-inch piece fresh ginger, peeled and sliced	2 tablespoons packed brown sugar
1 star anise, broken	3 tablespoons chopped fresh cilantro Clementines or tangerines, peeled and sectioned

1. Place a disposable slow cooker liner in a 5- to 6-quart ceramic slow cooker liner; set aside. Place ribs on a broiler pan. Sprinkle with salt and pepper. Broil 4 to 5 inches from the heat for 10 minutes or until browned. Place leeks in disposable liner; top with ribs. Add garlic, ginger, star anise, and dried chile pepper. In a medium bowl combine sherry, orange peel, orange juice, soy sauce, and brown sugar. Pour over ribs. Using a twist tie, close the disposable liner. Place the ceramic liner in the refrigerator overnight. (To serve today, cover and cook as directed in Step 2.)

2. Place ceramic liner in the slow cooker. Remove the twist tie from the disposable liner. Cover and cook on low-heat setting for 11 to 12 hours or on high-heat setting for 5½ to 6 hours.

3. Using a slotted spoon, transfer ribs to a platter; cover to keep warm. Strain cooking liquid; discard solids. Skim fat from cooking liquid. Sprinkle ribs with cilantro. Serve ribs with clementines and cooking liquid for dipping.

Per serving: *834 cal., 66 g fat (28 g sat. fat), 152 mg chol., 986 mg sodium, 20 g carb., 2 g fiber, 34 g pro.*

▶ italian pot roast

MAKE AHEAD UP TO 12 HOURS

PREP: 20 minutes   CHILL: up to 12 hours
COOK: 9 to 10 hours (low) or 4½ to 5 hours (high)   MAKES: 6 servings

  1   2½-pound boneless beef chuck pot roast
  1   teaspoon fennel seeds, toasted and crushed (see tip, page 52)
 ½   teaspoon garlic powder
 ½   teaspoon black pepper
  2   medium fennel bulbs, trimmed, cored, and cut into thin wedges
  3   medium carrots, halved lengthwise and cut diagonally into 2-inch pieces
  1   large onion, cut into thin wedges
  1   26-ounce jar tomato-basil pasta sauce
  6   ounces dried penne pasta
 ¼   cup snipped fresh Italian (flat-leaf) parsley

1. Place a disposable slow cooker liner in a 4- to 5-quart ceramic slow cooker liner. Trim fat from meat. For rub, in a small bowl stir together fennel seeds, garlic powder, and pepper. Sprinkle rub evenly over meat; rub in with your fingers. Place fennel, carrots, and onion in disposable liner. Place meat on vegetables. Using a twist tie, close the disposable liner. Place the ceramic liner in the refrigerator overnight. (To serve today, cover and cook as directed in Step 2.)

2. Place ceramic liner in the slow cooker. Remove the twist tie from the disposable liner. Pour pasta sauce over meat and vegetables. Cover and cook on low-heat setting for 9 to 10 hours or on high-heat setting for 4½ to 5 hours.

3. Cook pasta according to package directions; drain. Toss pasta with parsley. Using a slotted spoon, remove meat and vegetables from cooker. Using two forks, pull meat apart into large pieces. Skim fat from cooking liquid.

4. Serve meat, vegetables, and cooking liquid over pasta.

Per serving: *643 cal., 31 g fat (11 g sat. fat), 166 mg chol., 596 mg sodium, 44 g carb., 8 g fiber, 44 g pro.*

▶ spicy cuban flank steak sandwiches

MAKE AHEAD UP TO 12 HOURS

PREP: 20 minutes   CHILL: up to 12 hours
COOK: 8 to 9 hours (low) or 4 to 4½ hours (high)   MAKES: 10 servings

     1 **2-pound beef flank steak**
 1¼ **teaspoons onion powder**
 1¼ **teaspoons dried oregano, crushed**
 1¼ **teaspoons ground cumin**
 1¼ **teaspoons black pepper**
 1¼ **teaspoons granulated garlic**
     1 **teaspoon crushed red pepper**
  ½ **teaspoon salt**
     2 **large onions, cut into thin wedges**
 1¼ **cups 50% less sodium beef broth**
  ⅓ **cup lime juice**
   10 **Cuban rolls or French rolls, split**
     1 **recipe Picadillo Relish**

1. Place a disposable slow cooker liner in a 3½- or 4-quart ceramic slow cooker liner. Trim fat from meat. Cut meat crosswise into four pieces. For rub, in a small bowl stir together onion powder, oregano, cumin, black pepper, garlic, crushed red pepper, and salt. Sprinkle rub evenly over meat pieces; rub in with your fingers. Place meat in disposable liner. Add onions, broth, and lime juice. Using a twist tie, close the disposable liner. Place the ceramic liner in the refrigerator overnight. (To serve today, cover and cook as directed in Step 2.)

2. Place ceramic liner in the slow cooker. Remove the twist tie from the disposable liner. Cover and cook on low-heat setting for 8 to 9 hours or on high-heat setting for 4 to 4½ hours.

3. Remove meat from cooker. Using two forks, pull meat apart into coarse shreds. Return shredded meat to cooker; stir into cooking liquid. To serve, use a slotted spoon to spoon meat onto bottom halves of buns. Add Picadillo Relish and bun tops.

PICADILLO RELISH: In a large skillet heat 2 tablespoons oil over medium-high heat. Add 1½ cups chopped onions, ¾ cup chopped red sweet pepper, ¾ cup yellow sweet pepper, and 6 cloves garlic, minced. Cook and stir about 5 minutes or until vegetables are tender. Stir in one 15-ounce can black beans, rinsed and drained; 1 cup chopped tomatoes; ¼ cup chopped pitted green olives; ¼ cup chopped raisins; 3 tablespoons red wine vinegar; 1 teaspoon brown sugar; ¾ teaspoon ground cinnamon; and ¼ teaspoon crushed red pepper. Cook and stir for 2 minutes more. Cool to room temperature.

Per serving: *370 cal., 13 g fat (4 g sat. fat), 37 mg chol., 620 mg sodium, 38 g carb., 6 g fiber, 27 g pro.*

Prepare garnishes and toppings the night before then store them in airtight containers alongside the slow cooker ceramic liner.

▶ all-american sloppy joes

MAKE AHEAD UP TO 12 HOURS

PREP: 40 minutes   CHILL: up to 12 hours
COOK: 6 to 8 hours (low) or 3 to 4 hours (high)   MAKES: 16 servings

- 3 pounds lean ground beef or ground pork
- 2 cups chopped onions (2 large)
- 4 cloves garlic, minced
- 2½ cups chopped red sweet peppers
- 2 cups chopped celery (4 stalks)
- 1 12-ounce can beer
- 1 cup ketchup
- 2 tablespoons molasses
- 2 tablespoons yellow mustard
- 4 teaspoons chili powder
- 2 teaspoons cider vinegar
- Dash bottled hot pepper sauce
- 16 whole grain hamburger buns or kaiser rolls, split and toasted
- Dill pickle slices and/or pickled jalapeño pepper slices (optional)

1. Place a disposable slow cooker liner in a 3½- or 4-quart ceramic slow cooker liner; set aside. In an extra-large skillet cook ground beef, onions, and garlic over medium-high heat until meat is browned and onions are tender. Drain off fat. Cool meat slightly.

2. Place cooked meat mixture in disposable liner. Add sweet peppers, celery, beer, ketchup, molasses, mustard, chili powder, vinegar, and hot pepper sauce. Using a twist tie, close the disposable liner. Place the ceramic liner in the refrigerator overnight. (To serve today, cover and cook as directed in Step 3.)

3. Place ceramic liner in the slow cooker. Remove the twist tie from the disposable liner. Cover and cook on low-heat setting for 6 to 8 hours or on high-heat setting for 3 to 4 hours.

4. Using a slotted spoon, spoon meat onto bottom halves of buns. If desired, top with dill pickle and/or pickled jalapeño slices and bun tops.

Per serving: *399 cal., 16 g fat (5 g sat. fat), 58 mg chol., 575 mg sodium, 41 g carb., 3 g fiber, 23 g pro.*

This big-yield recipe is make-ahead in more ways than one. It cooks in the slow cooker well ahead of serving time—plus, leftovers can be refrigerated or frozen for another meal (or two).

▶ beef chili mac

MAKE AHEAD UP TO 12 HOURS

PREP: 25 minutes   CHILL: up to 12 hours   COOK: 4 to 6 hours (low) or 2 to 3 hours (high)
MAKES: 6 servings

1½ pounds ground beef
  1 cup chopped onion (1 large)
  3 cloves garlic, minced
  1 15-ounce can chili beans in chili gravy, undrained
  1 14.5-ounce can diced tomatoes and green chiles, undrained
  1 cup beef broth
¾ cup chopped green sweet pepper (1 medium)
  2 teaspoons chili powder
  1 teaspoon ground cumin
¼ teaspoon salt
  8 ounces dried cavatappi or macaroni
     Tortilla chips or corn chips
     Shredded cheddar cheese (optional)

1. Place a disposable slow cooker liner in a 3½- or 4-quart ceramic slow cooker liner; set aside. In a large skillet cook ground beef, onion, and garlic over medium heat until meat is browned and onion is tender, using a wooden spoon to break up meat as it cooks. Drain off and discard fat.

2. Place meat mixture, undrained chili beans, undrained tomatoes and green chiles, broth, sweet pepper, chili powder, cumin, and salt in disposable liner. Using a twist tie, close the disposable liner. Place the ceramic liner in the refrigerator overnight. (To serve today, cover and cook as directed in Step 3.)

3. Place ceramic liner in the slow cooker. Remove the twist tie from the disposable liner. Cover and cook on low-heat setting for 4 to 6 hours or on high-heat setting for 2 to 3 hours.

4. Cook pasta according to package directions. Stir cooked pasta into chili. Serve with tortilla chips. If desired, top with cheese.

Per serving: *559 cal., 22 g fat (7 g sat. fat), 77 mg chol., 871 mg sodium, 57 g carb., 8 g fiber, 33 g pro.*

▶ meatball sliders

MAKE AHEAD UP TO 12 HOURS

PREP: 15 minutes   CHILL: up to 12 hours   COOK: 4 to 5 hours (low) or 2 to 2½ hours (high)
MAKES: 12 servings

- 1 large red onion, cut into thin wedges
- 1 12-ounce package frozen cooked Italian-style meatballs (24 total)
- 1 24- to 26-ounce jar marinara sauce or tomato-base pasta sauce (about 2¼ cups)
- 1 tablespoon balsamic vinegar
- ½ teaspoon crushed red pepper
- 12 cocktail buns or Slider Buns,* split and, if desired, toasted
- 6 slices provolone cheese (6 ounces), halved
- 4 roma tomatoes, sliced

1. Place a disposable slow cooker liner in a 3½- or 4-quart ceramic slow cooker liner. Place onion wedges in disposable liner; top with frozen meatballs. In a medium bowl combine marinara sauce, vinegar, and crushed red pepper. Pour sauce over meatballs. Using a twist tie, close the disposable liner. Place the ceramic liner in the refrigerator overnight. (To serve today, cover and cook as directed in Step 2.)

2. Place ceramic liner in the slow cooker. Remove the twist tie from the disposable liner. Cover and cook on low-heat setting for 4 to 5 hours or on high-heat setting for 2 to 2½ hours. Gently stir meatballs and sauce in cooker.

3. To serve, layer bottom of each bun with half slice of cheese and two tomato slices. Top each with two meatballs, some of the sauce, and bun top.

*SLIDER BUNS: Thaw one 16-ounce loaf frozen white bread dough according to package directions. Preheat oven to 350°F. Cut loaf into 12 equal portions; shape each piece into a ball. Brush each bun with lightly beaten egg white; sprinkle with sesame seeds, poppy seeds, or dried herbs. Cover and let rise 45 to 60 minutes or until doubled in size. Bake for 12 to 15 minutes or until golden. Cool on a wire rack.

Per serving: 266 cal., 14 g fat (6 g sat. fat), 22 mg chol., 721 mg sodium, 24 g carb., 3 g fiber, 12 g pro.

▶ beef and black bean chili

MAKE AHEAD UP TO 12 HOURS

PREP: 25 minutes   CHILL: up to 12 hours
COOK: 8 to 10 hours (low) or 4 to 5 hours (high)   MAKES: 8 servings

- 12 ounces ground beef
- 1 cup chopped onion (1 large)
- ¾ cup chopped green sweet pepper (1 medium)
- 3 cloves garlic, minced
- 2 15-ounce cans black beans, rinsed and drained
- 1 28-ounce can diced tomatoes, undrained
- ¾ cup beef broth
- 2 tablespoons unsweetened cocoa powder
- 2 tablespoons hot chili powder
- 1 tablespoon ground cumin
- 1 tablespoon smoked paprika
- Sliced green onions (optional)

1. Place a disposable slow cooker liner in a 3½- or 4-quart ceramic slow cooker liner; set aside. In a large skillet cook ground beef, onion, sweet pepper, and garlic over medium-high heat until meat is browned, using a wooden spoon to break up meat as it cooks. Drain off fat.

2. Place meat mixture in disposable liner. Stir in beans, tomatoes, broth, cocoa powder, chili powder, cumin, and paprika. Using a twist tie, close the disposable liner. Place the ceramic liner in the refrigerator overnight. (To serve today, cover and cook as directed in Step 3.)

3. Place ceramic liner in the slow cooker. Remove the twist tie from the disposable liner. Cover and cook on low-heat setting for 8 to 10 hours or on high-heat setting for 4 to 5 hours. If desired, sprinkle servings with green onions.

Per serving: 236 cal., 10 g fat (3 g sat. fat), 30 mg chol., 695 mg sodium, 23 g carb., 8 g fiber, 14 g pro.

▶ spaghetti sauce italiano

MAKE AHEAD UP TO 12 HOURS

PREP: 25 minutes   CHILL: up to 12 hours
COOK: 8 to 10 hours (low) or 4 to 5 hours (high)   MAKES: 6 servings

- 1 pound bulk Italian sausage or ground beef
- 1 cup chopped onion (1 large)
- 2 cloves garlic, minced
- 2 14.5-ounce cans diced tomatoes, undrained
- 1 6-ounce can tomato paste
- 2 4-ounce cans mushroom stems and pieces, drained
- 1 bay leaf
- 2 teaspoons dried Italian seasoning, crushed
- ½ teaspoon salt
- ¼ teaspoon black pepper
- 1 cup chopped green sweet pepper (1 large)
- 12 to 16 ounces dried spaghetti, cooked and drained
  Finely shredded or grated Parmesan cheese (optional)

1. Place a disposable slow cooker liner in a 3½- or 4-quart ceramic slow cooker liner; set aside. In a large skillet cook the sausage, onion, and garlic over medium heat until meat is browned and onion is tender, using a wooden spoon to break up meat as it cooks. Drain off and discard fat.

2. Place undrained tomatoes, tomato paste, mushrooms, bay leaf, Italian seasoning, salt, and black pepper in disposable liner. Stir in sausage mixture. Using a twist tie, close the disposable liner. Place the ceramic liner in the refrigerator overnight. (To serve today, cover and cook as directed in Step 3.)

3. Place ceramic liner in the slow cooker. Remove the twist tie from the disposable liner. Cover and cook on low-heat setting for 8 to 10 hours or on high-heat setting for 4 to 5 hours. Discard bay leaf. Stir in sweet pepper. Serve meat sauce over hot cooked spaghetti. If desired, sprinkle with Parmesan cheese.

Per serving: 553 cal., 23 g fat (10 g sat. fat), 51 mg chol., 1,506 mg sodium, 62 g carb., 6 g fiber, 27 g pro.

▶ cranberry-chipotle country-style ribs

MAKE AHEAD UP TO 12 HOURS

PREP: 15 minutes   CHILL: up to 12 hours
COOK: 7 to 8 hours (low) or 3½ to 4 hours (high)   MAKES: 6 servings

> 2½ to 3 pounds boneless pork country-style ribs
> Salt
> Black pepper
> 1 16-ounce can whole cranberry sauce
> 1 cup chopped onion (1 large)
> 3 canned chipotle peppers in adobo sauce, finely chopped (see tip, page 29)
> 3 cloves garlic, minced

1. Place a disposable slow cooker liner in a 3½- or 4-quart ceramic slow cooker liner; set aside. Trim fat from ribs. Sprinkle ribs with salt and black pepper. Place ribs in disposable liner. For sauce, in a medium bowl combine cranberry sauce, onion, chipotle peppers, and garlic. Pour sauce over ribs. Using a twist tie, close the disposable liner. Place the ceramic liner in the refrigerator overnight. (To serve today, cover and cook as directed in Step 2.)

2. Place ceramic liner in the slow cooker. Remove the twist tie from the disposable liner. Cover and cook on low-heat setting for 7 to 8 hours or on high-heat setting for 3½ to 4 hours.

3. Transfer ribs to a serving platter. Stir sauce. Drizzle some of the sauce over ribs. If desired, serve with remaining sauce.

Per serving: *395 cal., 10 g fat (4 g sat. fat), 139 mg chol., 247 mg sodium, 32 g carb., 2 g fiber, 40 g pro.*

Leftover canned chipotle peppers in adobo sauce freeze well. Divide into small portions and freeze in tightly sealed containers. Thaw at room temperature for 30 minutes before using.

▶ pork ribs and beans

MAKE AHEAD UP TO 12 HOURS

PREP: 20 minutes   CHILL: up to 12 hours
COOK: 8 to 9 hours (low) or 4 to 4½ hours (high)   MAKES: 6 servings

2 pounds boneless pork country-style
  ribs
1 teaspoon Italian seasoning, crushed
¾ teaspoon dried rosemary, crushed
¼ teaspoon black pepper
½ cup chopped onion (1 medium)
1 15- to 19-ounce can white kidney
  (cannellini) beans, rinsed and drained

1 15-ounce can black beans, rinsed
  and drained
1 14.5-ounce can no-salt-added diced
  tomatoes, undrained
¼ cup dry red wine or water
3 tablespoons shredded Parmesan
  cheese (optional)

1. Place a disposable slow cooker liner in a 3½- or 4-quart ceramic slow cooker liner; set aside. Trim fat from meat. Sprinkle ribs with Italian seasoning, rosemary, and pepper. Place meat in disposable liner. Add onion, beans, and tomatoes. Pour wine over all. Using a twist tie, close the disposable liner. Place the ceramic liner in the refrigerator overnight. (To serve today, cover and cook as directed in Step 2.)

2. Place ceramic liner in the slow cooker. Remove the twist tie from the disposable liner. Cover and cook on low-heat setting for 8 to 9 hours or on high-heat setting for 4 to 4½ hours.

3. Using a slotted spoon, transfer pork ribs and beans to a serving bowl. Spoon some of the cooking liquid over meat and beans. If desired, sprinkle each serving with Parmesan cheese.

Per serving: *325 cal., 8 g fat (3 g sat. fat), 111 mg chol., 415 mg sodium, 24 g carb., 8 g fiber, 41 g pro.*

**Seasoning meats with herbs or black pepper well in advance of cooking
time allows them to absorb the flavor.**

▶ pork shoulder in roasted tomato sauce

MAKE AHEAD UP TO 12 HOURS

PREP: 30 minutes   CHILL: up to 12 hours   COOK: 8 hours (low)   MAKES: 8 servings

- 1 2-pound boneless pork shoulder roast
- 8 ounces uncooked chorizo sausage, casings removed
- 2 cups cubed red-skinned potatoes (2 medium)
- 1 14.5-ounce can diced fire-roasted tomatoes, undrained
- 1 cup chopped onion (1 large)
- 3 canned chipotle peppers in adobo sauce, chopped (see tip, page 29)
- 1 tablespoon canned adobo sauce
- 2 bay leaves
- 4 cloves garlic, minced
- 1 teaspoon dried thyme, crushed
- 1 teaspoon dried Mexican oregano or regular oregano, crushed
- ½ teaspoon salt
- ¼ teaspoon sugar
- 1 10-ounce package tortilla chips or 16 corn tortillas, warmed
- 2 avocados, seeded, peeled, and thinly sliced
- 2 cups crumbled queso fresco (8 ounces)
- Fresh cilantro sprigs (optional)

1. Place a disposable slow cooker liner in a 3½- or 4-quart slow cooker ceramic slow cooker liner; set aside. Trim fat from pork roast. Cut roast into 1-inch pieces; set aside. In a large skillet cook sausage over medium-high heat until browned, using a wooden spoon to break up meat as it cooks. Remove sausage and drain on paper towels.

2. Place pork roast, sausage, potatoes, tomatoes, onion, chipotle peppers, adobo sauce, bay leaves, garlic, thyme, oregano, salt, and sugar in disposable liner. Using a twist tie, close the disposable liner. Place the ceramic liner in the refrigerator overnight. (To serve today, cover and cook as directed in Step 3.)

3. Place ceramic liner in the slow cooker. Remove the twist tie from the disposable liner. Cover and cook on low-heat setting for 8 hours.

4. Using a slotted spoon, remove pork roast from cooker. Using two forks, pull roast apart into coarse shreds. Remove and discard bay leaves. Skim fat from tomato sauce. Return shredded meat to cooker; stir to combine.

5. Serve meat and sauce in shallow bowls with tortilla chips. Top servings with avocado, queso fresco, and, if desired, cilantro.

Per serving: 661 cal., 37 g fat (12 g sat. fat), 119 mg chol., 1,022 mg sodium, 42 g carb., 6 g fiber, 41 g pro.

▶ cuban sandwiches with dilled cucumbers

MAKE AHEAD UP TO 12 HOURS

PREP: 30 minutes   CHILL: up to 12 hours
COOK: 8 to 9 hours (low) or 4 to 4½ hours + 30 minutes (high)   MAKES: 10 servings

- 1 2½- to 3-pound pork sirloin roast
- 1 teaspoon dry mustard
- ½ teaspoon ground cumin
- ½ teaspoon black pepper
- ½ cup water
- 1 recipe Dilled Cucumbers
- 3 medium orange, yellow, and/or red sweet peppers, thinly sliced crosswise
- 2 medium banana peppers, stemmed, seeded, and thinly sliced crosswise
- 2 tablespoons yellow mustard
- 5 whole grain ciabatta buns, split (about 12 ounces total)
- 4 ounces thinly sliced cooked lower-sodium ham

1. Place a disposable slow cooker liner in a 3½- or 4-quart ceramic slow cooker. Trim fat from roast; if necessary cut roast to fit slow cooker. In a small bowl combine dry mustard, cumin, and black pepper; evenly sprinkle on meat. Place meat in disposable liner. Using a twist tie, close the disposable liner. Place the ceramic liner in the refrigerator overnight. (To serve today, add the water to the cooker. Cover and cook as directed in Step 2.)

2. Place ceramic liner in the slow cooker. Remove the twist tie from the disposable liner. Add the water to the cooker. Cover and cook on low-heat setting for 8 to 9 hours or on high-heat setting for 4 to 4½ hours. Meanwhile, prepare Dilled Cucumbers. If using low-heat setting, turn to high-heat setting. Add sweet peppers and banana peppers to slow cooker. Cover and cook for 30 minutes more.

3. Remove pork from cooker. Using two forks, coarsely shred pork. Stir shredded pork into the cooking liquid in cooker.

4. Spread yellow mustard on split sides of ciabatta buns. Using a slotted spoon, divide pork among bun halves. Place ham on pork. Using a slotted spoon, remove peppers from cooker and spoon onto ham. Using a slotted spoon, top peppers with Dilled Cucumbers. If desired, drizzle some of the cucumber marinade on the sandwiches.

DILLED CUCUMBERS: For the marinade, in a large bowl whisk together ½ cup cider vinegar, ¼ cup light mayonnaise, 4 teaspoons snipped fresh dill (or 1 teaspoon dried dill), and ¼ teaspoon salt. Add 2 large English cucumbers, thinly sliced, and half of a red onion, cut into slivers, to the marinade. Toss to coat. Cover and chill for 2 to 4 hours before serving.

Per serving: *294 cal., 8 g fat (2 g sat. fat), 72 mg chol., 498 mg sodium, 25 g carb., 3 g fiber, 28 g pro.*

▶ vietnamese pork

MAKE AHEAD UP TO 12 HOURS

PREP: 25 minutes   CHILL: up to 12 hours
COOK: 10 to 12 hours (low) or 5 to 6 hours (high)   MAKES: 8 servings

- 2 fresh jalapeño chile peppers (see tip, page 29)
- 1 2½- to 3-pound boneless pork shoulder roast
- 2 tablespoons packed brown sugar
- ½ teaspoon black pepper
- 1 medium onion, cut into thin wedges
- 2 cloves garlic, minced
- ¼ cup water
- 2 tablespoons fish sauce
- 2 tablespoons lime juice
- 8 whole wheat flour tortillas, warmed*
- 4 cups mesclun
- 1 cup halved cucumber slices
- 1 recipe Pickled Carrots
- ¼ cup snipped fresh cilantro

1. Place a disposable slow cooker liner in a 3½- or 4-quart ceramic slow cooker liner; set aside. Cut one of the jalapeño peppers in half lengthwise. Thinly slice the remaining jalapeño pepper; wrap and chill sliced pepper until ready to serve.

2. Trim fat from meat. If necessary, cut meat to fit slow cooker. For rub, in a small bowl stir together brown sugar and pepper. Sprinkle rub evenly over meat; rub in with your fingers. Place meat in disposable liner. Add halved jalapeño pepper, onion, and garlic. Using a twist tie, close the disposable liner. Place the ceramic liner in the refrigerator overnight. (To serve today, cover and cook as directed in Step 3.)

3. Place ceramic liner in the slow cooker. Remove the twist tie from the disposable liner. In a small bowl stir together the water, fish sauce, and lime juice. Pour over pork mixture in cooker. Cover and cook on low-heat setting for 10 to 12 hours or on high-heat setting for 5 to 6 hours.

4. Using a slotted spoon, remove meat and onion from cooker; discard cooking liquid. Using two forks, pull meat apart into shreds. Stir onion into shredded meat.

5. Divide shredded meat among tortillas. Top with mesclun, cucumber, Pickled Carrots, cilantro, and reserved sliced jalapeño pepper.

PICKLED CARROTS: In a small nonreactive bowl stir together ½ cup warm water, 2 tablespoons white vinegar, 1 tablespoon sugar, and ½ teaspoon salt. Stir in 2 medium carrots, cut into thin bite-size strips. Cover and chill for at least 8 hours. Use a slotted spoon for serving.

Per serving: 362 cal., 7 g fat (2 g sat. fat), 85 mg chol., 966 mg sodium, 36 g carb., 3 g fiber, 37 g pro.

To warm tortillas, preheat oven to 350°F. Stack tortillas then wrap them tightly in foil. Warm for 10 minutes or until heated through.

▶ hungarian pork goulash

MAKE AHEAD UP TO 12 HOURS

PREP: 30 minutes   CHILL: up to 12 hours
COOK: 5 to 6 hours (low) or 2½ to 3 hours + 30 minutes (high)   MAKES: 6 servings

- 1 1½- to 2-pound pork sirloin roast
- 1 tablespoon Hungarian paprika or Spanish paprika
- 1 teaspoon caraway seeds, crushed
- ½ teaspoon garlic powder
- ½ teaspoon black pepper
- ¼ teaspoon salt
- 1 tablespoon canola oil
- 2 stalks celery, thinly sliced (1 cup)
- 2 medium carrots, thinly sliced (1 cup)
- 2 medium parsnips, halved lengthwise if large and thinly sliced (1 cup)
- 1 large onion, chopped (1 cup)
- 1 14.5-ounce can no-salt-added diced tomatoes, undrained
- ½ cup water
- 4 ounces dried wide whole grain noodles (2 cups dried)
- 6 tablespoons light sour cream
  Paprika (optional)

1. Place a disposable slow cooker liner in a 3½- or 4-quart ceramic slow cooker liner; set aside. Trim fat from roast. Cut roast into 2-inch cubes. In a large bowl combine the 1 tablespoon paprika, caraway seeds, garlic powder, pepper, and salt. Add pork cubes and toss to coat. In a large skillet cook pork, half at a time, in hot oil over medium heat until browned, turning occasionally. Place meat in disposable liner. Add celery, carrots, parsnips, onion, and tomatoes. Using a twist tie, close the disposable liner. Place the ceramic liner in the refrigerator overnight. (To serve today, place ingredients directly into ceramic liner and omit disposable liner. Add the water to the cooker. Cover and cook as directed in Step 2.)

2. Place ceramic liner in the slow cooker. Remove the twist tie from the disposable liner. Add the water to the cooker. Cover and cook on low-heat setting for 5 to 6 hours or for 2½ to 3 hours on high-heat setting.

3. If using low-heat setting, turn to high-heat setting. Stir noodles into goulash in cooker. Cover and cook on high-heat setting for 30 minutes or until noodles are tender, stirring once halfway through cooking. Top each serving with sour cream and, if desired, sprinkle with paprika.

Per serving: *285 cal., 9 g fat (2 g sat. fat), 82 mg chol., 234 mg sodium, 24 g carb., 5 g fiber, 28 g pro.*

Pasta and noodles can be cooked to just under al dente. Drain and store in a sealed container in the refrigerator up to 2 days. To reheat, drop in a pot of boiling water. Let stand for 1 to 2 minutes, then drain and serve.

▶ ham and sweet potato soup

MAKE AHEAD UP TO 12 HOURS

PREP: 20 minutes   CHILL: up to 12 hours
COOK: 5 to 6 hours (low) or 2½ to 3 hours (high)   MAKES: 6 servings

1½ **pounds sweet potatoes, peeled and cubed**
1 **15- or 19-ounce can cannellini (white kidney) beans, rinsed and drained**
1½ **cups cubed leftover cooked ham**
½ **cup chopped onion (1 medium)**
½ **teaspoon dried thyme, crushed**
¼ **teaspoon black pepper**
1 **32-ounce carton reduced-sodium chicken broth**
½ **cup half-and-half or light cream**
  Crème fraîche (optional)
  Paprika (optional)

1. Place a disposable slow cooker liner in a 3½- or 4-quart ceramic slow cooker liner. Place sweet potatoes, beans, ham, onion, thyme, and pepper in disposable liner. Add broth. Using a twist tie, close the disposable liner. Place the ceramic liner in the refrigerator overnight. (To serve today, place ingredients directly into ceramic liner and omit disposable liner. Cover and cook as directed in Step 2.)

2. Place ceramic liner in the slow cooker. Remove the twist tie from the disposable liner. Cover and cook on low-heat setting for 5 to 6 hours or on high-heat setting for 2½ to 3 hours. Stir in half-and-half.

3. Mash soup slightly with a potato masher to reach desired consistency. If desired, top servings with crème fraîche and/or paprika.

Per serving: 250 cal., 6 g fat (3 g sat. fat), 30 mg chol., 1,118 mg sodium, 36 g carb., 7 g fiber, 17 g pro.

▶ egg roll-style bowl

MAKE AHEAD UP TO 12 HOURS

PREP: 30 minutes   CHILL: up to 12 hours   COOK: 6 hours (low) or 3 hours (high)
MAKES: 8 servings

6	cups packaged shredded cabbage with carrot (coleslaw mix)
1¼	pounds lean ground pork, broken up
1	cup chopped bok choy or fresh spinach leaves
1	cup chopped red sweet pepper
½	cup finely chopped sweet onion (1 medium)
½	cup finely chopped celery (1 stalk)
¼	cup finely chopped green onions (2)
¼	cup soy sauce
3	tablespoons tomato paste
2	tablespoons red miso paste
2	tablespoons sake or cream sherry
1	tablespoon rice vinegar
1	teaspoon dried thyme, crushed
½	teaspoon salt
¼	teaspoon black pepper
4	cups reduced-sodium chicken broth

1. Place a disposable slow cooker liner in a 3½- or 4-quart ceramic slow cooker liner. Place coleslaw mix, ground pork, bok choy, sweet pepper, sweet onion, celery, green onions, soy sauce, tomato paste, miso paste, sake, vinegar, thyme, salt, and black pepper in disposable liner. Add broth. Using a twist tie, close the disposable liner. Place the ceramic liner in the refrigerator overnight. (To serve today, cover and cook as directed in Step 2.)

2. Place ceramic liner in the slow cooker. Remove the twist tie from the disposable liner. Cover and cook on low-heat setting for 6 hours or on high-heat setting for 3 hours.

Per serving: 247 cal., 15 g fat (6 g sat. fat), 51 mg chol., 1,215 mg sodium, 10 g carb., 2 g fiber, 16 g pro.

▶ italian braised chicken with fennel and cannellini

MAKE AHEAD UP TO 12 HOURS

PREP: 30 minutes   CHILL: up to 12 hours
COOK: 5 to 6 hours (low) or 2½ to 3 hours (high)   MAKES: 6 servings

- 2 to 2½ pounds chicken drumsticks and/or thighs, skin removed
- ¾ teaspoon salt
- ¼ teaspoon black pepper
- 1 15-ounce can cannellini beans (white kidney beans), rinsed and drained
- 1 14.5-ounce can diced tomatoes, undrained
- 1 fennel bulb, trimmed, cored, and cut into thin wedges
- 1 medium yellow sweet pepper, seeded and cut into 1-inch pieces
- 1 medium onion, cut into thin wedges

- ½ cup dry white wine or reduced-sodium chicken broth
- ¼ cup tomato paste
- 3 cloves garlic, minced
- 1 teaspoon snipped fresh rosemary or ½ teaspoon dried rosemary, crushed
- 1 teaspoon snipped fresh oregano or ½ teaspoon dried oregano, crushed
- ¼ teaspoon crushed red pepper
- ¼ cup shaved Parmesan cheese (1 ounce)
- 1 tablespoon snipped fresh Italian (flat-leaf) parsley

1. Place a disposable slow cooker liner in a 3½-or 4-quart ceramic slow cooker liner; set aside. Sprinkle chicken with ¼ teaspoon of the salt and the black pepper. Place chicken in disposable liner. In a large bowl combine beans, tomatoes, fennel, sweet pepper, onion, wine, tomato paste, garlic, rosemary, oregano, crushed red pepper, and the remaining ½ teaspoon salt; pour over chicken. Using a twist tie, close the disposable liner. Place the ceramic liner in the refrigerator overnight. (To serve today, cover and cook as directed in Step 2.)

2. Place ceramic liner in the slow cooker. Remove the twist tie from the disposable liner. Cover and cook on low-heat setting for 5 to 6 hours or on high-heat setting for 2½ to 3 hours.

3. Sprinkle servings with cheese and parsley.

Per serving: *223 cal., 4 g fat (1 g sat. fat), 68 mg chol., 762 mg sodium, 23 g carb., 7 g fiber, 25 g pro.*

It's always best to remove skin before cooking chicken in a slow cooker. To remove skin from chicken pieces, use a paper towel to grip the skin and pull it away from the meat. For drumsticks, start at the meaty end and pull toward the bony end. Use kitchen shears to cut skin at the joint, then wash shears in hot, soapy water.

▶ chicken ragoût

MAKE AHEAD UP TO 12 HOURS

PREP: 20 minutes   CHILL: up to 12 hours   COOK: 8 to 10 hours (low)   MAKES: 8 servings

8 chicken thighs, skinned (about 3½ pounds total)
2 14.5-ounce cans no-salt-added diced tomatoes, drained
3 cups 1-inch carrot slices or baby carrots
1 large onion, cut into wedges (1 cup)
⅓ cup reduced-sodium chicken broth
2 tablespoons white wine vinegar
1 teaspoon dried rosemary, crushed
1 teaspoon dried thyme, crushed
¼ teaspoon black pepper
8 ounces fresh button mushrooms, sliced
1 teaspoon olive oil
3 cups hot cooked whole wheat noodles
Snipped fresh basil or Italian (flat-leaf) parsley (optional)

1. Place a disposable slow cooker liner in a 3½- or 4-quart ceramic slow cooker liner. Place chicken thighs in slow cooker liner. In a large bowl stir together tomatoes, carrots, onion, broth, vinegar, rosemary, thyme, and pepper. Pour over chicken. Using a twist tie, close the disposable liner. Place the ceramic liner in the refrigerator overnight. (To serve today, cover and cook as directed in Step 2.)

2. Place ceramic liner in the slow cooker. Remove the twist tie from the disposable liner. Cover and cook on low-heat setting for 8 to 10 hours.

3. Just before serving, in a large nonstick skillet cook and stir mushrooms in hot oil over medium-high heat for 8 to 10 minutes or until golden. Remove chicken from cooker. Remove chicken from bones; discard bones. Stir chicken and mushrooms into ragoût in cooker. Serve ragoût over hot cooked noodles. If desired, sprinkle servings with basil.

Per serving: 234 cal., 4 g fat (1 g sat. fat), 57 mg chol., 163 mg sodium, 33 g carb., 7 g fiber, 20 g pro.

▶ chicken and vegetables with herbs

MAKE AHEAD UP TO 12 HOURS

PREP: 25 minutes   CHILL: up to 12 hours   COOK: 7 hours (low) or 3½ hours (high)
MAKES: 4 servings

    8 ounces fresh button mushrooms, halved
 1½ cups frozen small whole onions
  ½ cup reduced-sodium chicken broth
  ¼ cup dry red wine or reduced-sodium chicken broth
    2 tablespoons tomato paste
  ½ teaspoon garlic salt
  ½ teaspoon dried rosemary, crushed
  ½ teaspoon dried thyme, crushed
  ¼ teaspoon black pepper
    1 bay leaf
    8 small chicken thighs and/or drumsticks (about 2 pounds total), skinned
       Reduced-sodium chicken broth
  ¼ cup reduced-sodium chicken broth
    2 tablespoons flour
    3 cups hot cooked mashed potatoes (optional)
       Fresh Italian (flat-leaf) parsley sprigs (optional)

1. Place a disposable slow cooker liner in a 4- to 5-quart ceramic slow cooker liner. Place mushrooms and whole onions in disposable liner. Stir in the ½ cup broth, wine, tomato paste, garlic salt, rosemary, thyme, pepper, and bay leaf. Add chicken. Using a twist tie, close the disposable liner. Place the ceramic liner in the refrigerator overnight. (To serve today, cover and cook as directed in Step 2.)

2. Place ceramic liner in the slow cooker. Remove the twist tie from the disposable liner. Cover and cook on low-heat setting for 7 hours or on high-heat setting for 3½ hours.

3. Using a slotted spoon, transfer chicken and vegetables to a serving platter. Discard bay leaf. Cover chicken and vegetables to keep warm.

4. For sauce, skim fat from cooking liquid. Measure 1¾ cups of the cooking liquid, adding additional chicken broth, if necessary, to equal 1¾ cups total liquid. Transfer liquid to a medium saucepan. In a small bowl combine the ¼ cup broth and the flour until smooth; stir into liquid in saucepan. Cook and stir until thickened and bubbly; cook and stir for 1 minute more. Spoon some of the sauce over chicken. Pass remaining sauce. If desired, serve with mashed potatoes and sprinkle with parsley.

Per serving: 215 cal., 5 g fat (1 g sat. fat), 107 mg chol., 342 mg sodium, 10 g carb., 2 g fiber, 29 g pro.

Mashed potatoes can be made ahead and frozen, then thawed and reheated in the microwave. While mashed russets can get grainy when frozen, waxy, lower-starch potatoes—such as red potatoes—do not.

▶ jamaican jerk chicken sliders with pineapple salsa

MAKE AHEAD UP TO 12 HOURS

PREP: 30 minutes   CHILL: up to 12 hours
COOK: 7 to 8 hours (low) or 3½ to 4 hours + 30 minutes (high)   MAKES: 16 servings

2 tablespoons Jamaican jerk seasoning	Several dashes bottled hot pepper sauce
2 tablespoons olive oil	1½ cups finely chopped fresh pineapple
1 teaspoon kosher salt	¼ cup chopped green onions (2)
¾ teaspoon black pepper	¼ cup chopped red sweet pepper
3½ pounds bone-in chicken thighs, skin removed	2 tablespoons snipped fresh cilantro
1 cup brewed coffee	1 fresh jalapeño chile pepper, seeded and finely chopped (see tip, page 29) (optional)
¾ teaspoon finely shredded lime peel (set aside)	16 slider buns or small round dinner rolls, split and, if desired, toasted
3 tablespoons lime juice	
2 tablespoons molasses	
4 cloves garlic, minced	

1. Place a disposable slow cooker liner in a 3½- or 4-quart ceramic slow cooker liner. In a small bowl combine jerk seasoning, oil, salt, and black pepper. Coat chicken with seasoning mixture. Place chicken, bone sides down, in slow cooker liner.

2. In a small bowl combine coffee, 2 tablespoons of the lime juice, the molasses, garlic, and hot pepper sauce. Pour mixture over chicken. Using a twist tie, close the disposable liner. Place the ceramic liner in the refrigerator overnight. (To serve today, cover and cook as directed in Step 3.)

3. Place ceramic liner in slow cooker. Remove twist tie. Cover and cook on low-heat setting for 7 to 8 hours or on high-heat setting for 3½ to 4 hours.

4. Using a slotted spoon, remove chicken from cooker. When chicken is cool enough to handle, remove meat from bones; discard bones. Using two forks, pull chicken apart into shreds. Return shredded chicken to cooker. If using low-heat setting, turn to high-heat setting. Cover and cook about 30 minutes more or until heated through.

5. Meanwhile, for salsa, in a medium bowl stir together pineapple, green onions, sweet pepper, cilantro, jalapeño pepper (if desired), the remaining 1 tablespoon lime juice, and lime peel.

6. To serve, using a slotted spoon, divide chicken among buns. Top with salsa.

Per serving: 188 cal., 6 g fat (1 g sat. fat), 48 mg chol., 429 mg sodium, 19 g carb., 1 g fiber, 14 g pro.

▶ jalapeño chicken breasts

MAKE AHEAD UP TO 12 HOURS

PREP: 15 minutes   CHILL: up to 12 hours
COOK: 5 to 6 hours (low) or 2½ to 3 hours + 15 minutes (high)   MAKES: 6 servings

- 6 bone-in chicken breast halves, skinned
- 1 tablespoon chili powder
- ⅛ teaspoon salt
- ½ cup reduced-sodium chicken broth
- 2 tablespoons lemon juice
- ⅓ cup sliced pickled jalapeño chile pepper, drained
- 1 tablespoon cornstarch
- 1 tablespoon cold water
- 1 8-ounce package reduced-fat cream cheese (Neufchâtel), softened and cut into cubes
- 2 slices bacon, crisp-cooked, drained, and crumbled (optional)

1. Place a disposable slow cooker liner in a 4½- to 6-quart ceramic slow cooker liner; set aside. Sprinkle chicken with chili powder and salt. Arrange chicken, bone sides down, in disposable liner. Pour broth and lemon juice around chicken. Add drained jalapeño pepper. Using a twist tie, close the disposable liner. Place the ceramic liner in the refrigerator overnight. (To serve today, cover and cook as directed in Step 2.)

2. Place ceramic liner in the slow cooker. Remove the twist tie from the disposable liner. Cover and cook on low-heat setting for 5 to 6 hours or on high-heat setting for 2½ to 3 hours.

3. Transfer chicken and jalapeños to a serving platter, reserving cooking liquid in slow cooker. Cover chicken and keep warm.

4. If using low-heat setting, turn to high-heat setting. For sauce, in a small bowl, combine cornstarch and the 1 tablespoon water; stir into cooking liquid. Add cream cheese, whisking until combined. Cover and cook 15 minutes more or until thickened. Serve chicken with sauce. If desired, sprinkle servings with bacon.

Per serving: *329 cal., 11 g fat (6 g sat. fat), 143 mg chol., 489 mg sodium, 5 g carb., 1 g fiber, 49 g pro.*

▶ indian curry chicken

MAKE AHEAD UP TO 12 HOURS

PREP: 25 minutes   CHILL: up to 12 hours
COOK: 8 to 10 hours (low) or 4 to 5 hours + 15 minutes (high)   MAKES: 5 servings

5	medium white potatoes (about 1½ pounds), peeled
1	medium green sweet pepper, seeded and cut into 1-inch pieces
1	medium onion, sliced
1	pound skinless, boneless chicken breast halves or thighs, cut into 1-inch pieces
1½	cups chopped tomatoes (3 medium)
1	tablespoon ground coriander
1½	teaspoons paprika
1	teaspoon grated fresh ginger or ¼ teaspoon ground ginger
¾	teaspoon salt
½	teaspoon ground turmeric
¼ to ½	teaspoon crushed red pepper
¼	teaspoon ground cinnamon
⅛	teaspoon ground cloves
1	cup chicken broth
2	tablespoons cold water
4	teaspoons cornstarch

1. Place a disposable slow cooker liner in a 5- to 6-quart ceramic slow cooker liner. Place potatoes, sweet pepper, and onion in disposable liner. Add chicken.

2. In a medium bowl combine tomatoes, coriander, paprika, ginger, salt, turmeric, crushed red pepper, cinnamon, and cloves; stir in broth. Pour over chicken in cooker. Using a twist tie, close the disposable liner. Place the ceramic liner in the refrigerator overnight. (To serve today, cover and cook as directed in Step 3.)

3. Place ceramic liner in the slow cooker. Remove the twist tie from the disposable liner. Cover and cook on low-heat setting for 8 to 10 hours or on high-heat setting for 4 to 5 hours.

4. If using low-heat setting, turn to high-heat setting. In a small bowl combine the 2 tablespoons water and cornstarch; stir into liquid in cooker. Cover and cook for 15 to 20 minutes more or until slightly thickened and bubbly.

Per serving: *246 cal., 2 g fat (0 g sat. fat), 53 mg chol., 609 mg sodium, 31 g carb., 5 g fiber, 26 g pro.*

TIP

Freeze grated fresh ginger to keep it fresh and to punch up the flavor of a dish at a moment's notice. Place teaspoon-size portions of grated or minced fresh ginger on a parchment lined baking sheet, then freeze. When portions are solid, transfer to a resealable plastic bag and freeze until needed.

▶ new potato, broccoli, and chicken casserole

MAKE AHEAD UP TO 12 HOURS

PREP: 30 minutes   CHILL: up to 12 hours   COOK: 6 to 7 hours + 30 minutes (low)
MAKES: 6 servings

- 1 10.75-ounce can condensed cream of broccoli soup or cream of asparagus soup
- 1 8-ounce carton sour cream
- 1½ cups shredded Gruyère cheese or Swiss cheese (6 ounces)
- ½ cup milk
- 1 teaspoon dried Italian seasoning, crushed
- ¼ teaspoon black pepper
- 6 cups cubed red-skinned tiny new potatoes
- 3 cups chopped cooked chicken
- 2 cups broccoli florets
- ½ cup snipped fresh basil
  Shredded Gruyère cheese or Swiss cheese (optional)

1. Place a disposable slow cooker liner in a 4- to 5-quart ceramic slow cooker liner. Place soup and sour cream in disposable liner. Stir in the 1½ cups shredded cheese, milk, Italian seasoning, and pepper. Stir in potatoes and chicken. Using a twist tie, close the disposable liner. Place the ceramic liner in the refrigerator overnight. (To serve today, cover and cook as directed in Step 2.)

2. Place ceramic liner in the slow cooker. Remove the twist tie from the disposable liner. Cover and cook on low-heat setting for 6 to 7 hours. Stir in broccoli. Cover and cook 30 minutes more.

3. To serve, stir about half the basil into the casserole. Sprinkle with additional cheese, if desired, and the remaining basil.

Per serving: 520 cal., 26 g fat (13 g sat. fat), 122 mg chol., 559 mg sodium, 36 g carb., 4 g fiber, 37 g pro.

Because fresh basil leaves are very delicate, stir them into long-simmered dishes or sauces right before serving. Otherwise, the tender leaves bruise and discolor easily and the flavor breaks down quickly with extended heat.

▶ chicken and veggie burritos

MAKE AHEAD UP TO 12 HOURS

PREP: 25 minutes   CHILL: up to 12 hours
COOK: 6 to 7 hours (low) or 3 to 3½ hours + 30 minutes (high)
STAND: 5 minutes   MAKES: 8 servings

 1 large green sweet pepper, cubed
 1 cup coarsely chopped onion (1 large)
 1 cup coarsely chopped celery (2 stalks)
 1½ pounds skinless, boneless chicken breast halves, cut into ½-inch-wide strips
 1 8-ounce bottle green taco sauce
 1 teaspoon instant chicken bouillon granules
 ½ teaspoon ground cumin
 2 medium zucchini, cut in half lengthwise
 ½ cup uncooked instant rice
 8 9- to 10-inch spinach, chile, or plain flour tortillas, warmed (see tip, below)
 1 cup chopped tomatoes (2 medium)
 ¾ cup shredded Monterey Jack cheese with jalapeño peppers (3 ounces)
 ¼ cup sliced green onions (2)

1. Place a disposable slow cooker liner in a 3½- or 4-quart ceramic slow cooker liner. Place sweet pepper, onion, and celery in disposable liner. Top with chicken. In a small bowl combine taco sauce, bouillon granules, and cumin. Pour over chicken. Using a twist tie, close the disposable liner. Place the ceramic liner in the refrigerator overnight. (To serve today, cover and cook as directed in Step 2.)

2. Place ceramic liner in the slow cooker. Remove the twist tie from the disposable liner. Cover and cook on low-heat setting for 6 to 7 hours or on high-heat setting for 3 to 3½ hours. Cut zucchini into ½-inch slices. Stir into chicken mixture in cooker. Cover and cook for 30 minutes more. Stir in uncooked rice. Cover and let stand for 5 minutes.

3. To serve, divide chicken and veggie filling among warmed tortillas. Top with tomatoes, cheese, and green onions. Fold bottom edge of each tortilla over filling; fold in opposite sides just until they meet.

Per serving: 328 cal., 8 g fat (3 g sat. fat), 59 mg chol., 603 mg sodium, 35 g carb., 3 g fiber, 27 g pro.

To warm tortillas, preheat oven to 350°F. Stack tortillas and wrap tightly in foil. Bake for 10 minutes of until heated through.

▶ easy tostadas

MAKE AHEAD UP TO 12 HOURS

PREP: 15 minutes   CHILL: up to 12 hours
COOK: 4 to 5 hours (low) or 2 to 2½ hours (high)   MAKES: 6 servings

    12 tostada shells
     4 cups shredded cooked chicken
     1 14.4-ounce package frozen sweet pepper and onion stir-fry vegetables
     2 10-ounce cans enchilada sauce
     1 cup shredded Mexican four-cheese blend (4 ounces)
    1½ cups shredded cabbage (optional)
        Sour cream, sliced avocado, and/or snipped fresh cilantro (optional)

1. Place a disposable slow cooker liner in a 3½- to 4-quart ceramic slow cooker liner. Coarsely break up six of the tostada shells. Place broken tostada shells, chicken, frozen vegetables, and enchilada sauce in disposable liner. Using a twist tie, close the disposable liner. Place the ceramic liner in the refrigerator overnight. (To serve today, cover and cook as directed in Step 2.)

2. Place ceramic liner in the slow cooker. Remove the twist tie from the disposable liner. Cover and cook on low-heat setting for 4 to 5 hours or on high-heat setting for 2 to 2½ hours.

3. Divide chicken mixture among the remaining six tostada shells. Top with cheese and, if desired, cabbage, sour cream, avocado, and/or cilantro.

Per serving: 421 cal., 20 g fat (7 g sat. fat), 101 mg chol., 807 mg sodium, 25 g carb., 2 g fiber, 34 g pro.

Cooked chicken is a time-saver in the kitchen. Prepare it ahead of time then refrigerate up to 3 days or freeze up to 3 months.

▶ corn chowder

MAKE AHEAD UP TO 12 HOURS

PREP: 15 minutes   CHILL: up to 12 hours   COOK: 6 to 8 hours (low) or 3 to 4 hours (high)
MAKES: 6 servings

    2 14.75-ounce cans cream-style corn
    1 pound red-skinned potatoes (3 medium), finely chopped
    1 14.5-ounce can seasoned chicken broth with roasted garlic
    1 11-ounce can whole kernel corn with sweet peppers, drained
    1 4-ounce can diced green chile peppers, undrained
    ¼ teaspoon black pepper
       Cracked black pepper (optional)
       Saltine crackers (optional)

1. Place a disposable slow cooker liner in a 3½- or 4-quart ceramic slow cooker liner. Place cream-style corn, potatoes, broth, corn with sweet peppers, green chile peppers, and black pepper in disposable liner. Using a twist tie, close the disposable liner. Place the ceramic liner in the refrigerator overnight. (To serve today, cover and cook as directed in Step 2.)

2. Place ceramic liner in the slow cooker. Remove the twist tie from the disposable liner. Cover and cook on low-heat setting for 6 to 8 hours or on high-heat setting for 3 to 4 hours.

3. If desired, top each serving with cracked black pepper and serve with crackers.

Per serving: 202 cal., 1 g fat (0 g sat. fat), 1 mg chol., 898 mg sodium, 49 g carb., 5 g fiber, 5 g pro.

▶ mexican meatball stew

MAKE AHEAD UP TO 12 HOURS

PREP: 10 minutes   CHILL: up to 12 hours
COOK: 6 to 7 hours (low) or 3 to 3½ hours (high)   MAKES: 8 servings

- 2 14.5-ounce cans Mexican-style stewed tomatoes, undrained
- 2 12-ounce packages frozen cooked Italian-style turkey meatballs, thawed (24 total)
- 1 15-ounce can black beans, rinsed and drained
- 1 14-ounce can seasoned chicken broth with roasted garlic
- 1 10-ounce package frozen whole kernel corn, thawed
- Fresh oregano (optional)

1. Place a disposable slow cooker liner in a 4- to 5-quart ceramic slow cooker liner. Place undrained tomatoes, thawed meatballs, drained beans, broth, and corn in disposable liner. Using a twist tie, close the disposable liner. Place the ceramic liner in the refrigerator overnight. (To serve today, cover and cook as directed in Step 2.)

2. Place ceramic liner in the slow cooker. Remove the twist tie from the disposable liner. Cover and cook on low-heat setting for 6 to 7 hours or high-heat setting for 3 to 3½ hours. If desired, sprinkle each serving with oregano.

Per serving: 287 cal., 13 g fat (6 g sat. fat), 37 mg chol., 1,134 mg sodium, 30 g carb., 6 g fiber, 16 g pro.

▶ vegetable casserole

MAKE AHEAD UP TO 12 HOURS

PREP: 20 minutes   CHILL: up to 12 hours
COOK: 4 to 6 hours (low) or 2 to 2½ hours (high)   STAND: 5 minutes   MAKES: 8 servings

- 2 19-ounce cans cannellini beans (white kidney beans), rinsed and drained
- 1 19-ounce can garbanzo beans (chickpeas) or fava beans, rinsed and drained
- ½ cup chopped onion (1 medium)
- ¼ cup basil pesto
- 4 cloves garlic, minced
- 1½ teaspoons dried Italian seasoning, crushed
- 1 16-ounce package refrigerated cooked plain polenta, cut in ½-inch-thick slices
- 2 cups finely shredded Italian blend cheeses (8 ounces)
- 1 large tomato, thinly sliced
- 2 cups fresh spinach
- 1 cup torn radicchio
- 1 tablespoon water

1. Place a disposable slow cooker liner in a 4- to 5-quart ceramic slow cooker liner. In a large bowl combine beans, onion, 2 tablespoons of the pesto, the garlic, and Italian seasoning. Layer half of the bean mixture, half of the polenta, and half of the cheese in the disposable liner. Add remaining beans mixture and polenta. Using a twist tie, close the disposable liner. Place the ceramic liner in the refrigerator overnight. (To serve today, cover and cook as directed in Step 2.)

2. Place ceramic liner in the slow cooker. Remove the twist tie from the disposable liner. Cover and cook on low-heat setting for 4 to 6 hours or on high-heat setting for 2 to 2½ hours. Add tomato, the remaining cheese, the spinach, and radicchio. In a small bowl combine the remaining 2 tablespoons pesto and the 1 tablespoon water. Drizzle pesto mixture over casserole. Let stand, uncovered, for 5 minutes before serving.

Per serving: 360 cal., 12 g fat (6 g sat. fat), 26 mg chol., 926 mg sodium, 46 g carb., 10 g fiber, 21 g pro.

▶ squash enchilada casserole

MAKE AHEAD UP TO 12 HOURS

PREP: 35 minutes   CHILL: up to 12 hours
COOK: 8 to 10 hours (low) or 4 to 5 hours + 50 minutes (high)
STAND: 20 minutes   MAKES: 4 servings

 2 cups chopped, peeled, and seeded butternut squash or acorn squash
 1 15.5-ounce can hominy, rinsed and drained
 1 15-ounce can black beans, rinsed and drained
 1 cup chopped onion (1 large)
 ¾ cup chopped red sweet pepper (1 medium)
 ½ cup salsa
 1 4-ounce can diced green chile peppers
 4 cloves garlic, minced
 ¼ teaspoon salt
 1 10-ounce can enchilada sauce
 1 8.5-ounce package corn muffin mix
 1 cup shredded Monterey Jack cheese with jalapeño chile peppers (4 ounces)
 ⅓ cup milk
 1 egg, lightly beaten
    Sour cream and/or snipped fresh cilantro (optional)

1. Place a disposable slow cooker liner in a 3½- or 4-quart ceramic slow cooker liner. Place squash, hominy, black beans, onion, sweet pepper, salsa, chile peppers, garlic, and salt in the disposable liner. Pour enchilada sauce over all. Using a twist tie, close the disposable liner. Place the ceramic liner in the refrigerator overnight. (To serve today, cover and cook as directed in Step 2.)

2. Place ceramic liner in the slow cooker. Remove the twist tie from the disposable liner. Cover and cook on low-heat setting for 8 to 10 hours or on high-heat setting for 4 to 5 hours.

3. For dumplings, in a medium bowl stir together corn muffin mix, ½ cup of the cheese, milk, and egg; stir just until combined. If using low-heat setting, turn to high-heat setting. Stir vegetable mixture. Spoon corn muffin batter on top of vegetable mixture in four to six mounds. Cover and cook for 50 minutes more or until a wooden toothpick inserted in the center of dumplings comes out clean (do not lift cover during cooking).

4. Sprinkle the remaining ½ cup cheese over dumplings. Turn off cooker. Let stand, uncovered, for 20 minutes before serving. If desired, serve with sour cream and sprinkle with fresh cilantro.

Per serving: *660 cal., 23 g fat (10 g sat. fat), 91 mg chol., 2,276 mg sodium, 95 g carb., 16 g fiber, 25 g pro.*

Supermarkets increasingly cater to busy cooks. Cut-up vegetables, such as butternut squash, are packaged and ready to use.

jump-start ▶
RECIPES

Assemble these recipes nearly to the point of cooking, then cover and refrigerate until ready to heat and eat. Or prep and chill the ingredients for a main-dish salad or noodle bowl, then toss together right before serving.

recipes ▸ HOURS AHEAD ▸▸ DAY OR DAYS AHEAD

▶▶ italian sausage-stuffed beef tenderloin

MAKE AHEAD UP TO 2 DAYS

PREP: 40 minutes   STAND: 15 minutes   CHILL: up to 2 days   ROAST: 50 minutes at 425°F
MAKES: 10 servings

- 1 ½-ounce package dried porcini mushrooms
- 2 tablespoons olive oil
- 2 large onions, quartered and thinly sliced
- 8 ounces bulk mild Italian sausage
- 2 cloves garlic, minced
- 4 cups coarsely chopped Swiss chard
- ½ cup finely shredded Parmesan cheese (2 ounces)
- ½ teaspoon kosher salt
- ½ teaspoon dried Italian seasoning, crushed
- ¼ teaspoon cracked black pepper
- 1 4-pound center-cut beef tenderloin, trimmed of fat
- 1 tablespoon olive oil
- 1 to 2 teaspoons kosher salt
- 1 teaspoon cracked black pepper

1. Rinse dried mushrooms; place in a small bowl. Add enough boiling water to cover; let stand for 20 minutes. Drain; squeeze dry. Chop mushrooms; set aside.

2. For the sausage filling, in a large skillet heat the 2 tablespoons oil over medium heat. Add onions; cook and stir for 5 to 6 minutes or until golden. Add sausage, garlic, and mushrooms; cook until sausage is browned, using a wooden spoon to break up meat as it cooks. Add chard; cook and stir until wilted. Spoon sausage filling into a colander set in a bowl. Using a wooden spoon, press to remove excess liquid. Discard liquid.

3. Spoon sausage filling into a medium bowl. Stir in Parmesan cheese, the ½ teaspoon salt, Italian seasoning, and the ¼ teaspoon pepper.

4. Cut beef tenderloin in half horizontally, cutting to but not through the opposite side. Open tenderloin like a book. Evenly spread the sausage filling over cut sides of the tenderloin. Bring up sides of tenderloin to enclose sausage filling. Using 100-percent-cotton kitchen string, tie the tenderloin together at 3-inch intervals. (To serve today continue as directed in Step 6.)

5. To refrigerate to serve later, wrap stuffed tenderloin tightly in plastic wrap. Refrigerate up to 2 days. Let stand at room temperature for 30 minutes before roasting.

6. Preheat oven to 425°F. If chilled, remove plastic wrap. Place tenderloin on the rack of a roasting pan, placing the stuffing slit to one side. Brush tenderloin with the 1 tablespoon olive oil; sprinkle with the 1 teaspoon salt and the 1 teaspoon pepper. Roast tenderloin to desired doneness. Allow 50 to 60 minutes for medium rare (145°F) or 65 to 70 minutes for medium (160°F). Transfer to a wire rack; tent loosely with foil. Let stand at room temperature for 15 minutes before carving. Discard string. Thickly slice tenderloin; serve immediately.

Per serving: 614 cal., 45 g fat (17 g sat. fat), 138 mg chol., 652 mg sodium, 9 g carb., 1 g fiber, 42 g pro.

▶▶ argentinean rolled flank steak

MAKE AHEAD UP TO 2 DAYS

PREP: 40 minutes   CHILL: up to 2 days   STAND: 40 minutes   GRILL: 40 minutes
MAKES: 6 servings

- 1 1¼- to 1½-pound beef flank steak
- 2 medium Anaheim chile peppers, seeded and chopped (see tip, page 29)
- ½ cup chopped sweet onion (1 medium)
- 2 cloves garlic, minced
- 1 tablespoon vegetable oil
- 1 tablespoon snipped fresh oregano
- ½ teaspoon salt
- ¼ teaspoon black pepper
- 4 ounces sliced cooked Black Forest ham or regular ham
- ½ cup shredded fontina cheese (2 ounces)
- 1 recipe Chimichurri Sauce
- 12 6-inch corn tortillas or 7- to 8-inch flour tortillas

1. Trim fat from meat. Score both sides of meat in a diamond pattern by making shallow diagonal cuts at 1-inch intervals. Place meat between two pieces of plastic wrap. Using the flat side of a meat mallet, pound meat lightly to about a 12×8-inch rectangle. Remove plastic wrap.

2. In a large skillet cook Anaheim peppers, onion, and garlic in hot oil over medium heat about 3 minutes or until tender, stirring occasionally. Stir in oregano, salt, and black pepper.

3. Arrange ham slices evenly on meat. Spread ham with pepper mixture; sprinkle with cheese. Starting from a long side, roll up rectangle. Tie in three or four places with heavy 100-percent-cotton kitchen string. (To serve today, continue as directed in Step 6.)

4. To refrigerate to serve later, wrap meat roll in plastic wrap. Refrigerate up to 2 days. Meanwhile, prepare Chimichurri Sauce; transfer to an airtight container. Cover and chill until needed.

5. To serve, let meat stand at room temperature for 30 minutes. Remove plastic wrap.

6. For a charcoal grill, arrange medium-hot coals around a drip pan. Test for medium heat above pan. Place meat on grill rack over drip pan. Cover and grill for 40 to 45 minutes or until an instant-read thermometer registers 150°F, turning once halfway through grilling. (For a gas grill, preheat grill. Reduce heat to medium. Adjust for indirect cooking. Cover and grill as above.)

7. Remove meat from grill. Cover with foil; let stand for 10 minutes. (Temperature of meat after standing should be 155°F.) Remove and discard string. Cut rolled steak into 1-inch slices. Serve with Chimichurri and tortillas.

CHIMICHURRI: In a food processor or blender combine 1¼ cups fresh Italian (flat-leaf) parsley leaves, ¼ cup olive oil, 1 medium shallot, 2 tablespoons fresh oregano leaves, 2 tablespoons red wine vinegar, 1 tablespoon lemon juice, 4 cloves garlic, ½ teaspoon salt, and ½ teaspoon crushed red pepper. Cover and process just until chopped and a few parsley leaves are visible. Cover and chill for 2 hours before serving.

Per serving: 631 cal., 28 g fat (7 g sat. fat), 61 mg chol., 1,273 mg sodium, 58 g carb., 1 g fiber, 36 g pro.

▶▶ short rib ragu with polenta croutons

MAKE AHEAD UP TO 3 DAYS

PREP: 45 minutes   BAKE: 2 hour 15 minutes at 325°F/1 hour at 375°F
COOL: 30 minutes   CHILL: 8 hours to 3 days   MAKES: 8 servings

- 3 pounds boneless beef short ribs
  Salt
  Black pepper
- 2 to 3 tablespoons olive oil
- 2 medium onions, thinly sliced
- 6 cloves garlic, minced
- 3 medium carrots, halved lengthwise and sliced (1½ cups)
- 1 cup coarsely chopped celery (2 stalks)
- 1 14-ounce can reduced-sodium beef broth
- 1½ cups dry red wine, such as Merlot or Cabernet Sauvignon
- 1 6-ounce can tomato paste
- 4 sprigs fresh thyme
- 1 8-ounce package cremini mushrooms, quartered (thickly slice large caps)
- 1 recipe Firm Polenta
- 1 tablespoon snipped fresh Italian parsley or basil (optional)

1. Preheat oven to 325°F. Sprinkle ribs with salt and pepper. In a 6- to 8-quart oven-going Dutch oven heat 1 tablespoon of the olive oil over medium heat. Brown ribs, half at a time if necessary, in the hot oil, turning to brown all sides; remove ribs and set aside. In the same Dutch oven cook onions and garlic for 2 minutes, adding another 1 tablespoon of the oil if needed. Add carrots and celery; cook about 5 minutes more or until vegetables are tender.

2. Return ribs to Dutch oven with the vegetables. Stir in broth, wine, tomato paste, and thyme sprigs. Bring to boiling. Cover; bake for 1½ hours. Stir in mushrooms. Bake, uncovered, for 45 to 60 minutes more or until ribs are tender and sauce is slightly thickened. Cool for 30 minutes. Discard thyme sprigs. Season to taste with additional salt and pepper.

3. Transfer short rib ragu to a large airtight container; cover. Chill at least 8 hours or up to 3 days.

4. Preheat oven to 375°F. Lightly grease a 3-quart rectangular baking dish; set aside. Using a spoon, remove any fat from surface of the sauce. Spoon ribs and sauce into prepared baking dish. If desired, cut short ribs into smaller portions. Run a thin metal spatula around the edges of the Firm Polenta in the loaf pan. Remove polenta loaf from pan and cut into 1-inch cubes. Arrange cubes evenly over the ribs and sauce in the baking dish. Brush the cubes with the remaining 1 tablespoon olive oil. Bake, uncovered, about 1 hour or until ribs and sauce are heated through and polenta is lightly browned. If desired, sprinkle with parsley.

FIRM POLENTA: In a medium saucepan bring 2½ cups water to boiling. Meanwhile, in a medium bowl stir together 1 cup coarse ground yellow cornmeal, 1 cup cold water, and 1 teaspoon salt. Slowly add cornmeal mixture to the boiling water, stirring constantly. Cook and stir until mixture returns to boiling. Reduce heat to medium-low. Cook for 25 to 30 minutes or until polenta is very thick and tender, stirring frequently and adjusting heat as necessary to maintain a slow boil. Pour into an 8×4×2-inch loaf pan, spreading evenly. Cover and chill at least 8 hours (up to 3 days).

Per serving: *593 cal., 41 g fat (16 g sat. fat), 86 mg chol., 716 mg sodium, 26 g carb., 3 g fiber, 22 g pro.*

▶▶ braciole-style flank steak

MAKE AHEAD UP TO 2 DAYS

PREP: 45 minutes   ROAST: 20 minutes at 425°F   STAND: 15 minutes   CHILL: up to 2 days
BAKE: 1½ hours at 350°F   MAKES: 4 servings

2 yellow sweet peppers	¼ cup dried currants
1½ teaspoons olive oil	2 tablespoons pine nuts, toasted (see tip, page 52)
¼ cup diced pancetta	
½ cup finely chopped onion (1 medium)	¾ teaspoon salt
2 cloves garlic, minced	½ teaspoon black pepper
1 10-ounce package frozen chopped spinach, thawed, well drained, and pressed dry	1 1½- to 2-pound beef flank steak
	2 tablespoons olive oil
	1½ cups marinara sauce
¼ cup coarsely grated Pecorino Romano cheese	½ cup dry red wine

1. Preheat oven to 425°F. Line a baking sheet with foil. Cut sweet peppers in half lengthwise; remove stems, seeds, and membranes. Place pepper halves, cut sides down, on prepared baking sheet. Roast for 20 to 25 minutes or until charred and very tender. Bring foil up around peppers and fold edges to enclose. Let stand about 15 minutes or until cool enough to handle. Using a sharp knife, loosen edges of the skins; gently pull off the skins in strips and discard. Cut peppers into strips; set aside.

2. In a medium saucepan heat the 1½ teaspoons olive oil over medium-high heat. Add pancetta; cook until browned, stirring frequently. Add onion and garlic; cook and stir over medium heat for 3 minutes. Remove from heat. Add spinach, cheese, currants, pine nuts, ¼ teaspoon of the salt, and ¼ teaspoon of the black pepper. Set aside.

3. Place flank steak between two pieces of plastic wrap. Using the flat side of a meat mallet, pound lightly to ½-inch thickness. Remove top plastic wrap. Sprinkle steak with the remaining ½ teaspoon salt and the remaining ¼ teaspoon black pepper.

4. Arrange sweet pepper strips lengthwise along the center of the flank steak, leaving 3 to 4 inches uncovered on both sides. Spoon spinach mixture evenly over the pepper strips.

5. Starting with a long side, use bottom plastic wrap to guide flank steak over and around filling, making a long roll. Tie roll at 1½-inch intervals with 100-percent-cotton kitchen string. Tuck in the ends of the roll; using a long piece of string, tie roll lengthwise. (To serve today, continue as directed in Steps 7 through 9.)

6. To refrigerate to serve later, wrap meat roll in plastic wrap. Chill up to 2 days.

7. Preheat oven to 350°F. Unwrap meat roll. In an extra-large oven-going skillet or braising pan heat the 2 tablespoons olive oil over medium-high heat. Add meat roll; cook until browned on all sides, turning frequently.

8. In a small saucepan combine marinara sauce and wine. Cook over low heat just until boiling. Pour marinana-wine sauce over meat roll in skillet. Cover tightly. Bake about 1½ hours or until meat is fork-tender. Remove meat from skillet; remove strings and cut meat into 1-inch slices. Serve with the remaining sauce in skillet.

Per serving: 611 cal., 30 g fat (8 g sat. fat), 70 mg chol., 1,238 mg sodium, 33 g carb., 5 g fiber, 45 g pro.

▶▶ flank steak vinaigrette salad

MAKE AHEAD UP TO 2 DAYS

PREP: 20 minutes   GRILL: 15 minutes   CHILL: up to 2 days   MAKES: 4 servings

⅓ cup cider vinegar
3 tablespoons olive oil
2 tablespoons snipped fresh cilantro
1 to 2 teaspoons sugar
1½ teaspoons red wine vinegar
1 teaspoon coarse ground mustard
¼ teaspoon salt
⅛ teaspoon black pepper
¾ cup finely chopped green sweet
  pepper

¼ cup peeled and finely chopped jicama
2 tablespoons finely chopped red onion
½ of a fresh serrano chile pepper,
  seeded and chopped (see tip, page
  29)
8 ounces beef flank steak
12 ounces tiny new potatoes, quartered
8 ounces fresh sugar snap pea pods,
  trimmed (optional)
6 cups mixed salad greens

1. For cilantro-pepper vinaigrette, in a medium bowl whisk together cider vinegar, oil, cilantro, sugar, red wine vinegar, mustard, salt, and black pepper. Stir in sweet pepper, jicama, onion, and serrano chile pepper. Cover and chill up to 2 days.

2. Trim fat from meat. For a charcoal or gas grill, place meat on the grill rack directly over medium heat. Cover and grill for 15 to 17 minutes for medium (160°F), turning once halfway through grilling. Thinly slice meat; transfer to a medium bowl; cover and chill up to 2 days.

3. Shortly before serving time, in a large covered saucepan cook potatoes in enough lightly salted boiling water to cover for 10 minutes. Add pea pods. Cook for 1 minute more; drain. Rinse with cold water; drain again.

4. In an extra-large bowl combine salad greens and potato mixture. Pour ½ cup of the vinaigrette over meat; toss gently to coat. Pour the remaining vinaigrette over greens mixture; toss gently to coat.

5. To serve, transfer salad to a serving platter; top with meat.

Per serving: *210 cal., 15 g fat (3 g sat. fat), 26 mg chol., 225 mg sodium, 27 g carb., 5 g fiber, 17 g pro.*

▶ weeknight lasagna

MAKE AHEAD UP TO 24 HOURS

PREP: 30 minutes   BROIL: 12 minutes   CHILL: 2 to 24 hours   STAND: 40 minutes
BAKE: 30 minutes at 375°F   MAKES: 12 servings

- 2 **pounds zucchini (about 2 large or 3 medium)**
  Nonstick cooking spray
- 1 **pound 95% lean ground beef**
- 2 **cups chopped fresh portobello mushrooms**
- 2 **cloves garlic, minced**
- 1 **24- to 26-ounce jar chunky tomato-base pasta sauce**
- 1 **8-ounce can tomato sauce**
- 1 **teaspoon dried basil, crushed**
- 1 **teaspoon dried oregano, crushed**
- 1 **teaspoon fennel seeds, crushed**
- 1 **egg, lightly beaten**
- 1 **15-ounce container ricotta cheese**
- 2 **cups shredded mozzarella cheese (8 ounces)**

1. Preheat broiler. Trim ends off zucchini. Cut zucchini lengthwise into ¼-inch-thick slices. Lightly coat both sides of zucchini slices with cooking spray; place in a single layer on a wire rack set on a large baking sheet. Broil about 6 inches from the heat for 12 to 14 minutes or until lightly browned, turning once halfway through broiling.

2. For sauce, in a large skillet cook ground beef, mushrooms, and garlic over medium-high heat until meat is browned, using a wooden spoon to break up meat as it cooks. Drain off fat. Stir in pasta sauce, tomato sauce, basil, oregano, and fennel seeds. In a small bowl combine egg and ricotta cheese.

3. To assemble lasagna, spread 1 cup of the sauce in an ungreased 13×9×2-inch baking pan. Top with enough of the zucchini slices to cover sauce. Carefully spread half the ricotta mixture over zucchini in pan; sprinkle with ¾ cup of the mozzarella cheese. Spread half the remaining sauce over layers in pan. Top with the remaining zucchini, the remaining ricotta mixture, ¾ cup of the mozzarella cheese, and the remaining sauce. (To serve today, continue as directed in Step 5.)

4. To refrigerate to serve later, cover baking dish with plastic wrap, then with foil. Chill for 2 to 24 hours. To serve, let stand at room temperature for 30 minutes.

5. Preheat oven to 375°F. Remove plastic wrap; replace foil. Bake for 20 minutes. Sprinkle with the remaining ½ cup mozzarella cheese. Bake, uncovered, for 10 to 15 minutes more or until lasagna is heated through and cheese is melted. Let stand for 10 minutes before serving.

Per serving: *197 cal., 7 g fat (3 g sat. fat), 57 mg chol., 557 mg sodium, 14 g carb., 3 g fiber, 20 g pro.*

The zucchini "noodles" can be broiled up to 24 hours ahead of assembling the lasagna. Let cool, cover, and refrigerate until ready to use.

▶▶ kansas city beef soup

MAKE AHEAD UP TO 3 DAYS

PREP: 20 minutes   COOK: 20 minutes   CHILL: up to 3 days   HEAT: 30 minutes
MAKES: 6 servings

1½ pounds lean ground beef
1 cup chopped onion (1 large)
1 cup sliced celery (2 stalks)
2 14.5-ounce cans 50% less sodium beef broth
1 28-ounce can diced tomatoes, undrained
1 10-ounce package frozen mixed vegetables
2 tablespoons steak sauce
2 teaspoons Worcestershire sauce
¼ teaspoon salt
¼ teaspoon black pepper
¼ cup all-purpose flour
   Snipped fresh Italian (flat-leaf) parsley

1. In a large Dutch oven cook ground beef, onion, and celery over medium-high heat until meat is browned and vegetables are tender, using a wooden spoon to break up meat as it cooks. Drain off fat.

2. Stir in 1 can of the broth, the tomatoes, frozen vegetables, steak sauce, Worcestershire sauce, salt, and pepper. Bring to boiling; reduce heat. Simmer, covered, for 20 minutes.

3. In a medium bowl whisk together the remaining can of broth and the flour; stir into soup in Dutch oven. Cook over medium-high heat until thickened and bubbly. Cook and stir for 1 minute more. (To serve today, omit Steps 4 and 5. Serve as directed in Step 6.)

4. To refrigerate to serve later, cool soup slightly. Transfer soup to airtight containers. Cover and chill up to 3 days.

5. To serve, transfer chilled soup to a large Dutch oven. Cook over medium heat about 30 minutes or until heated through, stirring occasionally.

6. Ladle soup into soup bowls. Sprinkle each serving with parsley.

Per serving: *306 cal., 12 g fat (5 g sat. fat), 74 mg chol., 747 mg sodium, 21 g carb., 4 g fiber, 27 g pro.*

▶▶ sweet onion soup with porcini mushrooms

MAKE AHEAD UP TO 3 DAYS

PREP: 30 minutes   STAND: 15 minutes   COOK: 30 minutes   CHILL: up to 3 days
MAKES: 6 servings

1 ounce dried porcini mushrooms
2 cups boiling water
4 ounces pancetta
1 tablespoon butter or olive oil
1½ pounds sweet onions, such as Vidalia or Maui, sliced
4 cloves garlic, minced
1 tablespoon packed brown sugar

1 teaspoon salt
¼ cup Marsala wine
4 cups reduced-sodium beef broth
1 sprig fresh thyme
1 sprig fresh rosemary
1 bay leaf
1 recipe Toasted Cheese Bread (optional)

1. Place porcini mushrooms in a medium bowl. Pour the boiling water over mushrooms. Cover and let stand for 15 minutes. Meanwhile, in a 4-quart Dutch oven cook pancetta in hot butter over medium heat until lightly browned. Using a slotted spoon, remove pancetta; drain on paper towels, reserving drippings in Dutch oven. Chop pancetta; set aside.

2. Add sweet onions, garlic, brown sugar, and salt to the Dutch oven. Cook and stir over medium-low heat until golden, stirring occasionally.

3. Meanwhile, using a slotted spoon, remove porcini mushrooms from the liquid, reserving liquid. Chop mushrooms; set aside. Reserve all but ¼ cup of the mushroom liquid (discard liquid at bottom of bowl, which may be gritty).

4. When the onions are golden, stir in mushrooms and Marsala wine. Cook until most of the liquid has evaporated. Add the reserved mushroom liquid, the beef broth, thyme, rosemary, and bay leaf. Bring to boiling; reduce heat. Simmer, uncovered, about 30 minutes. Discard thyme and rosemary sprigs and the bay leaf. (To serve today, continue as directed in Step 7.)

5. Cool soup slightly; transfer to an airtight container. Chill up to 3 days. Place pancetta in a small airtight container. Chill up to 3 days.

6. To refrigerate to serve later, return soup to the Dutch oven. Bring to boiling over medium heat, stirring occasionally.

7. Remove soup from heat; stir in pancetta. If desired, serve with Toasted Cheese Bread.

Per serving: *158 cal., 8 g fat (3 g sat. fat), 18 mg chol., 1,118 mg sodium, 16 g carb., 2 g fiber, 6 g pro.*

TOASTED CHEESE BREAD: Preheat broiler. Place twelve ½-inch slices baguette-style French bread on a baking sheet. Broil 4 to 5 inches from heat for 1 to 2 minutes or until toasted. Turn bread slices; sprinkle with 1 cup shredded Gruyère cheese (4 ounces). Broil for 1 to 2 minutes more or until cheese is melted and lightly browned.

▶ cranberry-stuffed pork loin

MAKE AHEAD UP TO 24 HOURS

PREP: 35 minutes   CHILL: up to 24 hours   STAND: 25 minutes   ROAST: 1½ hours at 325°F
MAKES: 8 servings

- 1 tablespoon butter
- 1 large sweet onion, such as Vidalia or Maui, cut into thin wedges
- ¾ cup dried cranberries
- 2 tablespoons coarse-grain Dijon-style mustard
- 1 tablespoon honey
- 1 tablespoon snipped fresh sage
  Salt
  Black pepper
- 1 3½-pound boneless pork top loin roast (single loin)

1. For stuffing, in a large skillet melt butter over medium-low heat. Add onion. Cook, covered, for 13 to 15 minutes or until onion is tender, stirring occasionally. Uncover; cook and stir over medium-high heat for 3 to 5 minutes or until golden. Stir in dried cranberries, mustard, honey, and sage. Season to taste with salt and pepper.

2. Cut pork loin in half horizontally, cutting to but not through the opposite side. Open roast like a book. Evenly spoon stuffing on cut sides of the roast. Bring up sides of roast to enclose stuffing. Using 100-percent-cotton kitchen string, tie the roast together at 3-inch intervals. (To serve today, continue as directed in Steps 4 and 5.)

3. To refrigerate to serve later, wrap roast tightly in plastic wrap. Chill up to 24 hours. Let stand at room temperature for 15 minutes before roasting.

4. Preheat oven to 325°F. If chilled, remove plastic wrap. Sprinkle roast with additional salt and pepper. Place roast on a rack in a shallow roasting pan. Roast, uncovered, for 1½ to 2 hours or until an instant-read thermometer inserted into the center registers 150°F. Transfer to a rack; tent roast loosely with foil. Let stand for 10 minutes before slicing.

5. To serve, remove string; slice roast.

Per serving: *392 cal., 17 g fat (6 g sat. fat), 130 mg chol., 268 mg sodium, 13 g carb., 1 g fiber, 43 g pro.*

▶ fruit-filled pork tenderloin

MAKE AHEAD UP TO 24 HOURS

PREP: 35 minutes   STAND: 40 minutes   CHILL: up to 24 hours   ROAST: 25 minutes at 425°F
MAKES: 8 servings

- ½ **cup ruby port wine or pomegranate juice**
- ¾ **cup golden raisins**
- ¾ **cup dried cranberries**
- ⅔ **cup dried apricots, quartered**
- ¼ **teaspoon apple pie spice**
- 2 **14- to 18-ounce pork tenderloins**
- ½ **teaspoon salt**
- ¼ **teaspoon black pepper**
  Dinner rolls (optional)
  Coarse-grain, Dijon-style, or honey mustard (optional)

1. For stuffing, in a small saucepan bring port just to boiling. Remove from heat. Stir in raisins, dried cranberries, dried apricots, and apple pie spice. Cover and let stand for 15 minutes. Transfer mixture to a food processor. Cover and process for 10 to 15 seconds or until coarsely ground.

2. Make a lengthwise cut along the center of each tenderloin, cutting to but not through the opposite side. Spread open. Place each tenderloin between two pieces of plastic wrap. Using the flat side of a meat mallet, lightly pound meat from center to edges to slightly less than ½-inch thickness. Remove plastic wrap.

3. Divide fruit filling between meat portions, spreading to within ½ inch of edges. Starting from a long side, roll up each portion into a spiral. Tie at 2-inch intervals with 100-percent-cotton kitchen string. Sprinkle rolls with salt and pepper. (To serve today, continue as directed in Steps 5 and 6.)

4. To refrigerate to serve later, wrap each stuffed tenderloin tightly in plastic wrap. Chill up to 24 hours.

5. Preheat oven to 425°F. Meanwhile, remove plastic wrap. Place tenderloins on a rack in a shallow roasting pan; let stand at room temperature for 15 minutes. Roast for 25 to 35 minutes or until juices run clear and an instant-read thermometer inserted into meat registers 155°F. Remove from oven. Cover loosely with foil; let stand for 10 minutes before slicing. (Temperature of meat after standing should be 160°F.)

6. Remove and discard string. Cut tenderloins into ½-inch-thick slices. Serve warm. If desired, serve in dinner rolls with mustard.

Per serving: 241 cal., 2 g fat (1 g sat. fat), 64 mg chol., 199 mg sodium, 30 g carb., 2 g fiber, 22 g pro.

To serve chilled meat rolls, cool slightly then wrap each roll in plastic wrap. Chill up to 48 hours. Cut into ½-inch slices to serve.

▶ pancetta-stuffed pork chops

MAKE AHEAD UP TO 24 HOURS

PREP: 25 minutes   MARINATE: 4 to 24 hours   GRILL: 25 minutes   STAND: 5 minutes
MAKES: 4 servings

    4 bone-in pork loin chops or rib chops, cut 1¼ inches thick
    ½ cup olive oil
    3 tablespoons finely shredded lemon peel
    2 tablespoons finely snipped fresh rosemary
    4 cloves garlic, minced
    ½ teaspoon salt
    ½ teaspoon freshly black pepper
    1 cup chopped onion (1 large)
    2 ounces pancetta, finely chopped
    ½ cup soft bread crumbs
    2 teaspoons finely snipped fresh rosemary
    1 teaspoon snipped fresh oregano
    2 cloves garlic, minced
    1 tablespoon lemon juice
      Small fresh oregano leaves (optional)

1. Trim fat from chops. Make a pocket in each chop by cutting horizontally from the fat side almost to bone. Place chops in a resealable plastic bag set in an extra-large bowl. For marinade, in a small bowl combine oil, lemon peel, 2 tablespoons rosemary, 4 cloves garlic, salt, and pepper. Pour marinade over chops. Seal bag; turn to coat chops. Marinate in the refrigerator for 4 to 24 hours, turning bag occasionally.

2. For stuffing, in a large skillet cook and stir onion and pancetta over medium-high heat for 6 to 8 minutes or until pancetta is browned and crisp. Remove from heat. Stir in bread crumbs, 2 teaspoons rosemary, snipped oregano, and 2 cloves garlic. Stir in lemon juice.

3. Drain chops, discarding marinade. Spoon stuffing into pockets in chops; press tops of chops lightly to secure stuffing.

4. For a charcoal grill, arrange medium-hot coals around a drip pan. Test for medium heat above pan. Place chops on grill rack over drip pan. Cover and grill for 25 to 30 minutes or until chops are slightly pink in center and juices run clear (145°F.) (For a gas grill, preheat grill. Reduce heat to medium. Adjust for indirect cooking. Cover and grill as above.)

5. Let chops stand for 5 minutes before serving. If desired, garnish with oregano leaves.

Per serving: *621 cal., 47 g fat (10 g sat. fat), 127 mg chol., 677 mg sodium, 10 g carb., 2 g fiber, 39 g pro.*

**Buy meat in bulk when it's on sale, then freeze until ready to use.
Although it is safe to thaw, prepare in a recipe, and freeze again—meat
loses quality in both flavor and texture after being refrozen.**

▶ pork and noodle salad

MAKE AHEAD UP TO 24 HOURS

PREP: 20 minutes   CHILL: 2 to 24 hours   MAKES: 4 servings

- 4 ounces dried Chinese egg noodles or fine noodles, broken in half
- 1 recipe Soy-Sesame Vinaigrette
- ¾ pound fresh asparagus, trimmed and cut into 2-inch-long pieces, or one 10-ounce package frozen cut asparagus
- 2 carrots, cut into thin strips
- 8 ounces cooked lean pork, cut into thin strips
- Sliced green onions (optional)
- Sesame seeds (optional)

1. Cook pasta according to package directions; drain. Meanwhile, prepare Soy-Sesame Vinaigrette.

2. If using fresh asparagus, cook in a covered saucepan in a small amount of lightly salted boiling water for 4 to 6 minutes or until crisp-tender. (If using frozen asparagus, cook according to package directions.) Drain well.

3. In a large bowl combine noodles, asparagus, carrots, and pork. Cover and chill for 2 to 24 hours.

4. To serve, pour Soy-Sesame Vinaigrette over salad; toss gently to coat. If desired, sprinkle salad with green onions and sesame seeds.

SOY-SESAME VINAIGRETTE: In a screw-top jar combine ¼ cup reduced-sodium soy sauce, 2 tablespoons rice vinegar or cider vinegar, 1 tablespoon canola or vegetable oil, 1 tablespoon honey, and 1 teaspoon sesame oil. Cover and shake well to mix. Chill for 2 to 24 hours.

Per serving: *328 cal., 12 g fat (3 g sat. fat), 76 mg chol., 974 mg sodium, 31 g carb., 2 g fiber, 24 g pro.*

After assembling a salad, keep it covered with a lid or topped with plastic wrap in the refrigerator up to 24 hours. Unless directed by the recipe, avoid adding the dressing or vinaigrette until just before serving.

▶ potluck choucroute garni

MAKE AHEAD UP TO 24 HOURS

PREP: 45 minutes   CHILL: up to 24 hours   STAND: 10 minutes   BAKE: 1 hour 5 minutes at 350°F
MAKES: 12 servings

1½ cups apple juice, apple cider, or chicken broth
 3 tablespoons cornstarch
 3 tablespoons coarse-grain brown mustard
 1 tablespoon caraway seeds
 1 tablespoon snipped fresh rosemary
 ½ teaspoon cracked black pepper
 1 medium red onion, cut into very thin wedges
 4 cloves garlic, minced
 1 tablespoon olive oil or vegetable oil
 1 12-ounce bottle ale or beer
12 ounces fingerling potatoes or tiny new potatoes, quartered
 3 medium carrots, sliced
 2 7.5-ounce packages cooked, smoked boneless pork chops, cut into bite-size pieces, or two
    6-ounce packages Canadian-style bacon, cut into chunks
 1 pound cooked, smoked kielbasa, halved lengthwise and bias-sliced into 1-inch pieces
 2 medium cooking apples, such as Granny Smith or Jonagold, cored and cut into chunks
 1 14-ounce can sauerkraut, rinsed and squeezed dry
    Coarse-grain brown mustard (optional)

1. For the sauce, in a medium bowl stir together apple juice, cornstarch, the 3 tablespoons mustard, caraway seeds, rosemary, and pepper; set aside. In a medium saucepan cook onion and garlic in hot oil over medium heat for 4 minutes or until tender. Stir in ale and apple juice mixture. Cook and stir until thickened and bubbly. Cool for 10 minutes.

2. Meanwhile, in a large saucepan cook potatoes and carrots, covered, in a large amount of lightly salted boiling water about 10 minutes or until slightly tender but still firm. Drain; set aside.

3. In a 3-quart rectangular baking dish layer pork chops, kielbasa, potatoes and carrots, apples, and sauerkraut. Spoon sauce over sauerkraut. Cover tightly with foil. (To serve today, continue as directed in Step 5, except bake, covered, for 45 to 60 minutes or until potatoes are tender and center is hot.)

4. To refrigerate to serve later, cover with plastic wrap and chill up to 24 hours. Let stand at room temperature for 10 minutes before baking.

5. Preheat oven to 350°F. If chilled, remove plastic wrap and cover with foil. Bake, covered, for 65 to 70 minutes or until potatoes are tender and center is hot. If desired, serve with additional coarse-grain mustard.

Per serving: 289 cal., 15 g fat (5 g sat. fat), 49 mg chol., 654 mg sodium, 23 g carb., 3 g fiber, 14 g pro.

▶▶ memphis dry ribs

MAKE AHEAD UP TO 3 DAYS

PREP: 25 minutes   BAKE: 3 hours at 275°F   CHILL: up to 3 days   GRILL: 20 minutes
MAKES: 6 servings

- 4 pounds pork loin back ribs or meaty pork spareribs
- 3 tablespoons packed brown sugar
- 2 tablespoons smoked paprika or sweet paprika
- 2 teaspoons celery salt
- 2 teaspoons onion powder
- 1 teaspoon garlic powder

- 1 teaspoon dried thyme, crushed
- 1 teaspoon coarse black pepper
- ⅛ teaspoon cayenne pepper
- ½ cup apple juice
- ⅓ cup barbecue sauce
- ⅓ cup cider vinegar
- 2 cups hickory or oak wood chips*
- Barbecue sauce (optional)

1. Preheat oven to 275°F. Trim fat from ribs. Place ribs in a shallow roasting pan. For rub, in a small bowl stir together brown sugar, paprika, celery salt, onion powder, garlic powder, thyme, black pepper, and cayenne pepper. Reserve 1 tablespoon of the rub. Evenly sprinkle the remaining rub over both sides of ribs; rub in with your fingers.

2. Pour apple juice into pan around (not on) ribs. Cover pan with foil. Bake for 3 hours or until ribs are very tender. Remove ribs from roasting pan.

3. Meanwhile, for mop sauce, in a small bowl combine the ⅓ cup barbecue sauce and the vinegar. Stir in the 1 tablespoon reserved rub. (To serve today, continue as directed in Step 5, except grill ribs for 15 to 20 minutes.)

4. To serve later, cover ribs with foil and chill for up to 3 days. Transfer mop sauce to an airtight container and chill until needed.

5. For a charcoal grill, arrange medium-hot coals around a drip pan. Test for medium heat above pan. Sprinkle wood chips over coals. Brush ribs generously with mop sauce. Place ribs on grill rack over drip pan. Cover and grill for 20 to 25 minutes or until ribs are heated through. (For a gas grill, preheat grill. Reduce heat to medium. Adjust for indirect cooking. Cover and grill as above, adding wood chips according to the manufacturer's directions.) Serve ribs with remaining mop sauce and, if desired, additional barbecue sauce.

Per serving: *487 cal., 29 g fat (11 g sat. fat), 129 mg chol., 809 mg sodium, 18 g carb., 1 g fiber, 37 g pro.*

For the most smoke production, soak wood chips in enough water to cover for at least 1 hour before grilling.

▶ baked ham with sautéed pears and apples

MAKE AHEAD UP TO 24 HOURS

PREP: 25 minutes   COOK: 25 minutes   CHILL: up to 24 hours
ROAST: 1 hour 30 minutes at 325°F   MAKES: 16 servings

3 cups water
¾ cup sugar
⅓ cup honey
1 teaspoon red curry paste
3 tablespoons butter
4 medium ripe pears, cored and sliced

1 tablespoon finely chopped fresh ginger
4 medium red cooking apples, such as Rome, Jonathan, or Braeburn, cored and sliced
1 5- to 6-pound cooked ham (rump half)
Snipped fresh thyme

1. For glaze, in a large saucepan stir together the water, sugar, honey, and curry paste. Bring to boiling, stirring constantly to dissolve sugar. Boil gently, uncovered, for 25 to 30 minutes or until slightly thickened, stirring occasionally. Cool.

2. Meanwhile, for fruit, in a large skillet melt butter over medium-high heat. Add pears and ginger. Cook for 5 to 7 minutes or until pears begin to brown, gently stirring occasionally. Remove from skillet; keep warm. Add apples to skillet; cook for 5 to 7 minutes or until apples begin to brown, gently stirring occasionally. Combine apples with pears. Cool. (To serve today, continue as directed in Steps 4 and 5.)

3. To serve later, place glaze and fruit in separate airtight containers. Chill up to 24 hours.

4. Preheat oven to 325°F. In a large saucepan reheat glaze just until bubbly. Remove ½ cup of the glaze; set remaining glaze aside. Place ham on the rack of a roasting pan. Insert an oven-going meat thermometer into center of ham. Bake for 1½ to 2¼ hours or until thermometer registers 140°F. Brush ham with reserved ½ cup glaze during the last 20 minutes of baking.

5. Just before serving, in a large skillet stir fruit over medium heat just until heated through. To serve, arrange fruit on serving platter. Slice ham and arrange on platter with fruit. Drizzle ham and fruit with the remaining glaze. If desired, garnish with thyme sprigs.

Per serving: *343 cal., 14 g fat (5 g sat. fat), 82 mg chol., 930 mg sodium, 29 g carb., 2 g fiber, 28 g pro.*

Cooking apples keep their shape when exposed to heat better than the apples intended for applesauce or eating out of hand. Although one of the best cooking varieties is Granny Smith, you'll want red-skinned apples for this recipe.

▶▶ country-style ribs with sweet and tangy sauce

MAKE AHEAD UP TO 2 DAYS

PREP: 25 minutes   BAKE: 1 hour 45 minutes at 350°F   CHILL: up to 2 days   STAND: 30 minutes
GRILL: 10 minutes   MAKES: 4 servings

- 2 to 2½ pounds bone-in pork country-style ribs
- Salt
- Black pepper
- ½ cup chili sauce
- 2 tablespoons apple jelly
- 1 tablespoon vinegar
- 1 teaspoon prepared mustard
- 1 teaspoon Worcestershire sauce
- ¼ teaspoon chili powder
- 1 recipe Herbed-Dijon Marinated Veggies (optional)

1. Preheat oven to 350°F. Trim fat from ribs. Place ribs in a shallow foil-lined roasting pan. Sprinkle with salt and black pepper. Cover pan with foil.

2. Bake ribs 1¾ to 2 hours or until very tender. Carefully drain off fat in roasting pan.

3. Meanwhile, for the sweet and tangy sauce, in a small saucepan heat chili sauce and jelly over medium heat until jelly is melted, stirring occasionally. Stir in vinegar, mustard, Worcestershire sauce, and chili powder. (To serve today, continue as directed in Step 5.)

4. To serve later, cover ribs with foil and chill for up to 2 days. Transfer sauce to an airtight container. Chill until needed. Let ribs stand at room temperature for 30 minutes before grilling.

5. For a gas or charcoal grill, place ribs on the grill rack directly over medium heat. Cover and grill for 10 to 15 minutes or until ribs are browned, turning once halfway through grilling and brushing occasionally with sweet and tangy sauce. Serve ribs with remaining sauce and, if desired, Herbed-Dijon Marinated Veggies.

Per serving: *351 cal., 13 g fat (5 g sat. fat), 187 mg chol., 330 mg sodium, 0 g carb., 0 g fiber, 53 g pro.*

HERBED-DIJON MARINATED VEGGIES: In a large bowl whisk together 3 tablespoons dry white wine, such as Pinot Grigio or Sauvignon Blanc; 2 tablespoons snipped fresh basil; 2 tablespoons snipped fresh parsley; 1 tablespoon olive oil; 2 teaspoons snipped fresh thyme or oregano, or ½ teaspoon dried thyme or oregano, crushed; 2 teaspoons Dijon-style mustard, 1 clove minced garlic; and ¼ teaspoon salt. Add 1½ cups small fresh cremini mushrooms, 1 cup grape tomatoes or cherry tomatoes, 1 cup yellow and/or orange sweet pepper strips, and 1 small zucchini, quartered lengthwise and cut into 1-inch pieces. Toss gently to coat. Cover and marinate in the refrigerator for 4 to 24 hours, stirring once or twice. Let stand at room temperature for 30 to 60 minutes before serving. Using a slotted spoon, transfer vegetables to a serving bowl.

▶ new orleans-style muffuletta

MAKE AHEAD UP TO 24 HOURS

PREP: 20 minutes   CHILL: 4 to 24 hours   MAKES: 6 servings

- ½ cup coarsely chopped pitted ripe olives
- ½ cup chopped pimiento-stuffed green olives
- 1 tablespoon snipped fresh Italian (flat-leaf) parsley
- 2 teaspoons lemon juice
- ½ teaspoon dried oregano, crushed
- 1 tablespoon olive oil
- 1 clove garlic, minced
- 1 16-ounce ciabatta bread or French bread
- 6 lettuce leaves
- 3 ounces thinly sliced salami, pepperoni, or summer sausage
- 3 ounces thinly sliced cooked ham or turkey
- 6 ounces thinly sliced provolone, Swiss, or mozzarella cheese
- 1 to 2 medium tomatoes, thinly sliced
- ⅛ teaspoon coarse black pepper

1. For the olive relish, in a small bowl combine ripe olives, green olives, parsley, lemon juice, and oregano. Cover and chill at least 4 hours or up to 24 hours.

2. In a small bowl stir together oil and garlic; set aside. Cut bread in half horizontally. Using a spoon, hollow out the inside of the top half, leaving a ¾-inch shell.

3. Brush bottom half of bread with garlic oil. Layer with lettuce, meats, cheese, and tomatoes. Sprinkle tomatoes with pepper. Stir olive relish; mound on top of tomatoes. Layer top half of bread. Cut into six portions. To serve later, tightly wrap each portion in plastic wrap.

Per serving: 435 cal., 21 g fat (8 g sat. fat), 41 mg chol., 1,512 mg sodium, 43 g carb., 3 g fiber, 20 g pro.

To keep sandwich bread from getting soggy, layer tomatoes so they don't touch the bread directly.

LOW-CAL   FEEDS A CROWD   QUICK

▶ cuban griller

MAKE AHEAD UP TO 12 HOURS

PREP: 25 minutes   CHILL: 2 to 12 hours   GRILL: 30 minutes   MAKES: 8 servings

2	tablespoons yellow mustard
2	tablespoons mayonnaise
1	16-ounce loaf Cuban bread or ciabatta bread, cut in half horizontally
8	ounces thinly sliced cooked ham
4	ounces thinly sliced roast pork
4	ounces thinly sliced salami
10	lengthwise sandwich dill pickle slices
6	ounces sliced Swiss cheese
	Nonstick cooking spray

1. In a small bowl combine mustard and mayonnaise. Spread cut sides of bread with mustard-mayonnaise. Layer the bottom with ham, pork, and salami. Pat pickle slices dry with paper towels. Place pickles on meat; add cheese. Replace top of bread; press down firmly.

2. Coat a 24×18-inch sheet of heavy foil with cooking spray. Tightly wrap sandwich in the greased foil. Wrap in a second sheet of foil; place on a baking sheet. Place a heavy skillet (add cans of vegetables for more weight) on top of sandwich to press ingredients firmly together; chill for at least 2 hours or overnight.

3. For a gas or charcoal grill, place foil-wrapped sandwich on the grill rack directly over medium-low heat. Cover and grill for 30 minutes, turning sandwich every 5 minutes.

4. To serve, carefully remove sandwich from foil and cut into eight portions.

Per serving: 365 cal., 17 g fat (7 g sat. fat), 63 mg chol., 1,188 mg sodium, 30 g carb., 1 g fiber, 23 g pro.

▶ grilled italian foccacia sandwich

MAKE AHEAD UP TO 12 HOURS

PREP: 20 minutes   CHILL: 8 to 12 hours   GRILL: 20 minutes   MAKES: 8 servings

- 1 6-ounce jar quartered marinated artichoke hearts
- ¼ cup chopped roasted red sweet pepper
- 2 tablespoons chopped pitted ripe olives
- 1 12-inch focaccia
- 4 ounces thinly sliced capicola
- 4 ounces thinly sliced salami
- 2 ounces thinly sliced mortadella
- 4 ounces thinly sliced provolone or Swiss cheese

1. For the artichoke relish, drain artichoke hearts; pat dry with paper towels. Coarsely chop artichokes; pat dry again. In a small bowl combine artichokes, roasted peppers, and olives; set aside.

2. Cut foccacia in half horizontally. Layer the bottom with capicola, salami, and mortadella. Spoon artichoke relish over meat; top with cheese. Replace top of focaccia. Tightly wrap sandwich in foil and chill overnight.

3. For a charcoal or gas grill, place foil-wrapped sandwich on the grill rack directly over medium heat. Cover and grill for 20 to 25 minutes or until bread is toasted and cheese is melted, turning every 5 minutes during grilling.

4. To serve, carefully remove sandwich from foil and cut into eight wedges.

Per serving: 285 cal., 13 g fat (5 g sat. fat), 38 mg chol., 927 mg sodium, 27 g carb., 2 g fiber, 16 g pro.

▶ sweet peppers stuffed with applewood bacon risotto

MAKE AHEAD UP TO 12 HOURS

PREP: 30 minutes   COOK: 20 minutes   STAND: 5 minutes
CHILL: 2 to 12 hours   BAKE: 30 minutes at 375°F   MAKES: 6 servings

- 6 slices applewood bacon, coarsely chopped
- ½ cup chopped onion (1 medium)
- ¾ cup Arborio rice
- 1 14.5-ounce can reduced-sodium chicken broth
- ¾ cup dry white wine or reduced-sodium chicken broth
- 1 cup frozen peas, thawed
- ⅓ cup finely shredded Parmigiano-Reggiano cheese or Parmesan cheese
  Salt (optional)
  Black pepper (optional)
- 6 small or 3 large red, yellow, or green sweet peppers
- 1 tablespoon snipped fresh basil or Italian (flat-leaf) parsley (optional)

1. In a large saucepan cook bacon over medium heat until crisp. Drain; reserve 1 tablespoon of the bacon drippings in saucepan. Crumble bacon then set aside. Cook onion in reserved drippings until tender. Add rice; cook and stir for 2 minutes more. Carefully stir in broth and wine. Bring to boiling; reduce heat. Simmer, covered, for 20 minutes or until liquid is absorbed; remove saucepan from heat. Stir in bacon and peas. Let stand, covered, for 5 minutes. Stir in cheese. If desired, season to taste with salt and black pepper.

2. Meanwhile, halve large peppers lengthwise or cut tops off small peppers. Remove membranes and seeds.

3. Spoon risotto filling into peppers. Place filled peppers in a shallow baking dish. (To serve today, cover dish with foil. Continue as directed in Step 5.)

4. To serve later, cover dish with foil. Chill for 2 to 12 hours.

5. Preheat oven to 375°F. Bake, covered, for 30 to 45 minutes or until heated through. (If chilled, bake chilled peppers, covered, for 50 to 55 minutes or until heated through.) If desired, sprinkle with basil.

Per serving: 235 cal., 7 g fat (3 g sat. fat), 13 mg chol., 392 mg sodium, 28 g carb., 3 g fiber, 9 g pro.

▶▶ cream of roasted fennel soup

MAKE AHEAD UP TO 2 DAYS

PREP: 45 minutes   ROAST: 25 minutes at 375°F   CHILL: up to 2 days   MAKES: 8 servings

    1 large fennel bulb (1½ to 2 pounds)
    1 cup coarsely chopped white onion (1 large)
    1 tablespoon olive oil
    ½ teaspoon kosher salt
    2 14.5-ounce cans reduced-sodium chicken broth
    1 large russet potato, peeled and cut into ½-inch cubes
    1 cup half-and-half, light cream, or evaporated milk
    2 tablespoons grapefruit juice
    ¾ teaspoon ground cumin
       Ground white pepper
       Kosher salt
    1 tablespoon fennel seeds
       Croutons (optional)

1. Preheat oven to 375°F. Cut off and discard tough fennel stalks, reserving the feathery tops. Remove any wilted outer layers and cut a thin slice from base of bulb. Cut fennel bulb and tender stalks into ½-inch slices, removing core. Snip feathery tops; set aside.

2. In a 13×9×2-inch baking pan spread fennel slices and onion in an even layer. Drizzle with oil; sprinkle with the ½ teaspoon salt. Roast about 25 minutes or just until vegetables are tender.

3. Transfer roasted fennel and onion to a large saucepan. Add broth and potato. Bring to boiling; reduce heat. Simmer, covered, about 10 minutes or until potato is tender. Cool slightly.

4. Using a handheld immersion blender, blend fennel mixture until smooth. (Or transfer fennel mixture, one-third at a time, to a blender or food processor. Cover and blend or process until smooth. Transfer puree to a bowl. Repeat twice. Return all of the fennel puree to saucepan.) Stir in half-and-half, grapefruit juice, and cumin. Heat through. Season to taste with white pepper and additional salt.

5. Meanwhile, in a small skillet cook fennel seeds over medium-high heat about 3 minutes or until lightly browned and fragrant, stirring frequently. (To serve today, garnish as directed in Step 8.)

6. Cool soup slightly. Pour soup into an airtight container. Cover and chill up to 2 days. Place fennel tops and toasted fennel seeds in separate airtight containers. Cover and chill fennel tops up to 2 days; store fennel seeds at room temperature up to 2 days.

7. To serve, return soup to saucepan. Cook over medium heat until heated through, stirring occasionally.

8. Sprinkle hot soup with fennel tops and toasted fennel seeds. If desired, serve with croutons.

Per serving: 97 cal., 5 g fat (2 g sat. fat), 11 mg chol., 416 mg sodium, 10 g carb., 2 g fiber, 3 g pro.

▶ butternut squash bisque

MAKE AHEAD UP TO 24 HOURS

PREP: 40 minutes   COOK: 35 minutes   CHILL: up to 24 hours   MAKES: 8 servings

- 1   2½- to 3-pound butternut squash or three 12-ounce packages frozen cooked winter squash, thawed
- ¼   cup butter
- 1   large carrot, coarsely chopped
- ½   cup chopped onion (1 medium)
- ½   cup coarsely chopped celery (1 stalk)
- 2   cloves garlic, minced
- 2   large Braeburn or Gala apples, peeled, cored, and chopped
- 1   48-ounce box reduced-sodium chicken broth
- 1   cup apple cider or apple juice
- 2   canned chipotle peppers in adobo sauce, coarsely chopped (see tip, page 29)
- ½   cup sour cream
- 3   ounces smoked Gouda or smoked cheddar cheese, finely shredded
    Crumbled crisp-cooked bacon and/or shaved Gouda cheese (optional)

1. Peel, seed, and cube butternut squash. In a 6-quart Dutch oven melt butter over medium-high heat. Add fresh squash (if using), carrot, onion, celery, and garlic. Cook about 10 minutes or until vegetables are tender, stirring frequently. Add frozen squash (if using), apples, broth, cider, and chile peppers. Bring to boiling; reduce heat. Simmer, covered, about 25 minutes or until vegetables and apples are tender. Remove from heat; cool slightly.

2. Using a handheld immersion blender, blend soup, leaving about half of it chunky. (Or transfer about half the soup to a food processor or blender. Cover and process or blend until smooth. Return to Dutch oven.) Stir in sour cream. (To serve today, continue as directed in Step 5.)

3. To serve later, cool soup slightly and transfer to an airtight container. Cover and chill up to 24 hours.

4. To serve, return soup to Dutch oven. Gently reheat over low heat, stirring occasionally and making sure soup does not boil.

5. Remove from heat; add shredded Gouda cheese, stirring until melted. Top with bacon and/or shaved Gouda cheese.

Per serving: *213 cal., 11 g fat (7 g sat. fat), 30 mg chol., 655 mg sodium, 26 g carb., 3 g fiber, 6 g pro.*

Packaged cooked bacon is convenient but pricey. To have some on hand when needed, cook a batch and drain well on paper towels. Store slices between layers of clean paper towels in a resealable plastic bag in the refrigerator up to 1 week. To recrisp, heat in the microwave for 30 seconds to 1 minute; drain again.

▶▶ jerk drumsticks with grilled mango salsa

MAKE AHEAD UP TO 3 DAYS

PREP: 10 minutes   BAKE: 35 minutes at 375°F   CHILL: up to 3 days   GRILL: 25 minutes
MAKES: 4 servings

- 8 chicken drumsticks or thighs (2½ to 3 pounds total), skinned if desired
- ¼ teaspoon salt
- ¼ teaspoon black pepper
- 2 tablespoons Pickapeppa sauce
- 2 tablespoons Jamaican jerk seasoning
- 1 medium mango, halved, seeded, and peeled
- 1 red onion cut into ½-inch slices

- 1 fresh jalapeño chile pepper, halved and seeded (see tip, page 29)
- 1 tablespoon snipped fresh cilantro
- ½ teaspoon finely shredded lime peel
- 1 tablespoon lime juice
- 1 teaspoon honey
- ½ teaspoon ground coriander
- ¼ teaspoon salt
- Lime wedges (optional)

1. Preheat oven to 375°F. Place chicken in an ungreased 15×10×1-inch baking pan. Sprinkle with the ¼ teaspoon salt and pepper.

2. Bake, uncovered, for 35 to 40 minutes or until an instant-read thermometer registers 170°F. (Chicken will be cooked through, but not yet tender.) (To serve today, continue as directed in Steps 4 through 6.)

3. To serve later, cool chicken. Place chicken in an airtight container. Cover and chill for up to 3 days.

4. Brush chicken with Pickapeppa sauce. Sprinkle jerk seasoning evenly over chicken; rub in with your fingers.

5. For a charcoal grill, arrange medium-hot coals around a drip pan. Test for medium heat above pan. Place chicken, mango, red onion, and jalapeño pepper on grill rack over drip pan. Cover and grill for 25 to 30 minutes or until chicken is heated through and tender (175°F) and mango, onion, and jalapeño are tender and lightly charred, turning once halfway through grilling and removing items from grill as they are done. (For a gas grill, preheat grill. Reduce heat to medium. Adjust for indirect cooking. Place chicken on a rack in a roasting pan. Place roasting pan, mango, red onion, and jalapeño pepper on grill rack over burner that is turned off. Cover and grill as above.)

6. For salsa, when cool enough to handle, chop mango, red onion, and jalapeño pepper. In a medium bowl combine mango, onion, jalapeño pepper, cilantro, lime peel, lime juice, honey, coriander, and ¼ teaspoon salt. Serve chicken with salsa and, if desired, lime wedges.

Per serving: *351 cal., 16 g fat (4 g sat. fat), 154 mg chol., 928 mg sodium, 12 g carb., 1 g fiber, 37 g pro.*

▶ chicken and sweet potato-stuffed manicotti

MAKE AHEAD UP TO 24 HOURS

PREP: 40 minutes   COOK: 30 minutes   CHILL: up to 24 hours   BAKE: 45 minutes at 350°F
MAKES: 6 servings

- 1½ pounds sweet potatoes
- ¼ cup half-and-half, light cream, or whipping cream
- 2 tablespoons butter
- 2 tablespoons chopped fresh ginger
- 6 cloves garlic, sliced
- ½ teaspoon salt
- ¼ teaspoon black pepper
- 1½ cups chopped cooked chicken
- 12 dried manicotti shells
- 1 10-ounce carton savory garlic cream cheese for cooking
- ¼ cup milk
- ¼ cup grated Pecorino Romano cheese or Parmesan cheese
- 1 tablespoon snipped fresh chives or chopped green onion

1. For filling, in a large saucepan cook sweet potatoes, covered, in enough boiling water to cover about 30 minutes or until tender; drain. Cool slightly; peel. Return sweet potatoes to saucepan. Mash with a potato masher.

2. Meanwhile, in a small saucepan combine half-and-half, butter, ginger, and garlic; bring to boiling. Remove from heat. Cover and let stand for 15 minutes. Strain through a fine-mesh sieve; discard solids. Stir half-and-half mixture, salt, and pepper into mashed sweet potatoes. Stir in chicken; cover and set aside.

3. Cook manicotti according to package directions. Rinse with cold water; drain well. Lightly grease a 3-quart rectangular baking dish; set aside.

4. Using a small spoon, stuff each manicotti with a scant ⅓ cup of the filling. Place in the prepared dish. In a small bowl combine cream cheese for cooking and milk; spoon over manicotti. Sprinkle with cheese. Cover with foil. (To serve today, continue as directed in Step 6, except bake, covered, for 30 to 35 minutes or until heated through.)

5. To serve later, chill up to 24 hours.

6. Preheat oven to 350°F. If chilled, bake covered, for 45 minutes or until heated through. Sprinkle with chives.

Per serving: 420 cal., 14 g fat (8 g sat. fat), 70 mg chol., 713 mg sodium, 53 g carb., 4 g fiber, 22 g pro.

▶▶ pesto chicken and tomatoes

MAKE AHEAD UP TO 3 DAYS

PREP: 10 minutes   BAKE: 40 minutes at 375°F   CHILL: up to 3 days   GRILL: 6 to 8 minutes
MAKES: 4 servings

1 tablespoon olive oil	Black pepper
4 cloves garlic, minced	3 tablespoons butter, softened
6 roma tomatoes, halved lengthwise	3 tablespoons basil pesto
1½ to 2 pounds meaty chicken pieces (breast halves, thighs, and drumsticks)	2 tablespoons chopped walnuts, toasted (see tip, page 52)
Salt	2 tablespoons finely chopped kalamata olives (optional)

1. Preheat oven to 375°F. In a small bowl combine oil and garlic. Lightly brush tomato halves, then chicken pieces, with garlic oil. Discard remaining garlic oil.

2. Place chicken in an ungreased 15×10×1-inch baking pan. Sprinkle with salt and pepper. Bake, uncovered, for 40 to 45 minutes or until chicken is nearly cooked through (165°F for breasts; 175°F for thighs and drumsticks), turning once halfway through baking.

3. Meanwhile, in a small bowl stir together butter, pesto, walnuts, and, if desired, olives. (To serve today, continue as directed in Steps 5 and 6.)

4. To serve later, cool chicken. Place chicken, tomatoes, and pesto mixture in separate airtight containers. Chill for up to 3 days.

5. For a charcoal grill, arrange medium-hot coals around a drip pan. Test for medium heat above pan. Place chicken and tomatoes, cut sides down, on grill rack over drip pan. Cover and grill for 6 to 8 minutes or until chicken is no longer pink (170°F for breasts; 175°F for thighs and drumsticks) and tomatoes are heated through, turning once halfway through grilling. (For a gas grill, preheat grill. Reduce heat to medium. Adjust for indirect cooking. Place chicken on grill rack over burner that is turned off; place tomatoes on grill rack over heat. Cover and grill as above.)

6. Remove chicken and tomatoes from grill. Immediately spread chicken and cut sides of tomatoes with pesto mixture.

Per serving: *407 cal., 30 g fat (10 g sat. fat), 104 mg chol., 252 mg sodium, 7 g carb., 1 g fiber, 28 g pro.*

When basil is abundant in the garden or farmers' markets, make a batch of pesto. Divide among an ice cube tray and freeze until solid. Pop out of the tray into a plastic bag and store in the freezer until ready to use.

▶ maple-brined chicken with roasted vegetables

MAKE AHEAD 12 HOURS

PREP: 1 hour   BRINE: up to 12 hours   ROAST: 1 hour 45 minutes at 400°F
STAND: 15 minutes   MAKES: 6 servings

- 1 cup kosher salt
- ½ cup packed brown sugar
- 4 cups apple juice or apple cider
- 4 cups water
- 1 cup pure maple syrup
- 2 tablespoons stone ground Dijon-style mustard
- 1 5- to 6-pound roasting chicken
- 6 large carrots, cut into 2-inch chunks
- 2 large onions, cut into ½-inch slices
- 2 fennel bulbs, trimmed and cut into wedges
- 4 cloves garlic, peeled and halved
- 6 sprigs fresh thyme
- 3 tablespoons olive oil
- Salt
- Black pepper
- 1 medium orange, halved

1. For brine, in an extra-large stainless-steel stockpot combine the kosher salt and brown sugar; stir in apple juice, the water, maple syrup, and mustard. Cook and stir over medium-high heat until salt and sugar are completely dissolved. Remove from heat and cool to room temperature.

2. Remove giblets from chicken, if present (reserve for another use if desired). Rinse chicken inside and out with cool water. Place chicken in stockpot, making sure it is immersed in brine. Cover stockpot. Chill for 12 hours.

3. Meanwhile, in a resealable plastic bag combine carrots, onions, fennel, garlic, and two sprigs of the thyme; drizzle olive oil over vegetables. Seal bag; massage vegetables through bag to evenly coat with oil. Chill up to 12 hours.

4. Preheat oven to 400°F. Remove chicken from brine; discard brine. Pat chicken dry both inside and out with paper towels. Sprinkle chicken cavity with salt and pepper. Place orange halves and the remaining four sprigs thyme in cavity. Skewer neck skin to back. Tie legs to tail. Twist wing tips under back. Spread vegetables evenly in a roasting pan. Place chicken, breast side up, on top of vegetables.

5. Roast for 1¾ to 2¼ hours or until an instant-read thermometer inserted into center of an inside thigh muscle registers 180°F. Remove chicken and vegetables from oven. Tent loosely with foil; let stand for 15 minutes before carving.

6. Serve chicken with roasted vegetables.

Per serving: 692 cal., 44 g fat (12 g sat. fat), 191 mg chol., 405 mg sodium, 22 g carb., 6 g fiber, 50 g pro.

▶ chicken enchiladas adobo

MAKE AHEAD UP TO 24 HOURS

PREP: 40 minutes   CHILL: 2 to 24 hours   STAND: 30 minutes   BAKE: 25 minutes at 375°F
MAKES: 8 servings

- 1 **14.5-ounce can diced fire-roasted tomatoes, undrained**
- ¾ **cup water**
- ½ **cup chopped sweet onion (1 medium)**
- 1 **canned chipotle pepper in adobo sauce (see tip, page 29)**
- 1 **tablespoon canned adobo sauce (optional)**
- 1 **tablespoon snipped fresh cilantro**
- 1 **teaspoon ground cumin**
- ½ **teaspoon chili powder**
- ½ **teaspoon kosher salt or ¼ teaspoon regular salt**

- 1 **pound skinless, boneless chicken breast halves or thighs, cut into bite-size strips**
- 1 **tablespoon vegetable oil**
- ½ **cup corn and black bean salsa**
- ½ **cup sour cream**
- ½ **teaspoon finely shredded lime peel**
- 8 **multigrain or whole wheat flour tortillas**
- ¾ **cup shredded Chihuahua cheese or Monterey Jack cheese (3 ounces)**
- ½ **cup sliced green onions (4)**
- 1 **2.25-ounce can sliced pitted ripe olives, drained**

1. Lightly grease a 3-quart rectangular baking dish; set aside. For sauce, in a medium saucepan combine tomatoes, the water, sweet onion, chipotle pepper, adobo sauce (if desired), cilantro, cumin, chili powder, and half the salt. Bring to boiling; reduce heat. Simmer, uncovered, for 15 minutes; cool slightly. Transfer to a blender or food processor. Cover and blend or process until smooth.

2. For filling, in a large skillet cook and stir chicken in hot oil over medium-high heat until no longer pink. Drain off fat. Stir in salsa, sour cream, lime peel, and the remaining salt.

3. To assemble enchiladas, spread ½ cup of the sauce in the prepared baking dish. Spoon about 3 tablespoons of the filling onto each tortilla near an edge; roll up tortilla. Place enchiladas, seam sides down, on sauce in dish. (To serve today, spoon the remaining sauce over enchiladas. Cover baking dish with foil. Continue as directed in Step 6.)

4. To serve later, cover baking dish with foil. Transfer the remaining sauce to an airtight container; cover. Chill enchiladas and sauce for 2 to 24 hours.

5. To serve, let enchiladas and the remaining sauce stand at room temperature for 30 minutes. Spoon the sauce over enchiladas. Cover baking dish with foil.

6. Preheat oven to 375°F. Bake for 15 minutes; sprinkle with cheese. Bake, uncovered, for 10 to 15 minutes more or until heated through. Sprinkle with green onions and olives.

Per serving: 322 cal., 12 g fat (5 g sat. fat), 54 mg chol., 912 mg sodium, 34 g carb., 4 g fiber, 20 g pro.

▶ chicken, bacon, and cheddar submarines

MAKE AHEAD UP TO 12 HOURS

PREP: 25 minutes   GRILL: 22 minutes   BAKE: 15 minutes at 400°F   CHILL: up to 12 hours
MAKES: 8 servings

- 3 skinless, boneless chicken breast halves (about 12 ounces total)
- ¼ teaspoon garlic salt
- ¼ teaspoon black pepper
- 1 small red onion, cut in ½-inch slices
- 1 tablespoon olive oil
- 9 slices bacon
- ⅓ cup mayonnaise
- 1 tablespoon coarse-ground mustard
- 2 12-inch loaves baguette-style French bread
- 8 slices cheddar cheese

1. Sprinkle chicken with garlic salt and pepper. Brush both sides of onion slices with oil. For a gas or charcoal grill, place chicken and onion on the grill rack directly over medium heat. Cover and grill for 12 to 15 minutes or until chicken is no longer pink (170°F) and onion is tender and lightly charred, turning once halfway through grilling. Remove from grill and thinly slice chicken. Separate onion into rings.

2. Meanwhile, preheat oven to 400°F. Line a 15×10×1-inch baking pan with foil. Place bacon on the prepared baking pan. Bake for 15 minutes or until bacon is crisp (you do not need to turn the bacon). Remove from pan and drain on paper towels.

3. In a small bowl combine mayonnaise and mustard. Cut bread loaves in half horizontally. Hollow out the inside of each half, leaving a ¾-inch shell. Spread the insides of bread halves with mayonnaise-mustard. Layer the bottoms with sliced chicken, onion rings, bacon, and cheese. Replace the tops; press down firmly. Tightly wrap each sandwich in foil and chill overnight.

4. For a gas or charcoal grill, place foil-wrapped sandwiches on the grill rack directly over medium heat. Cover and grill for 10 minutes or until heated through, turning every 2 minutes.

5. To serve, cut each sandwich into four portions. Secure each portion with a wooden pick; remove wooden picks before eating.

Per serving: 623 cal., 25 g fat (9 g sat. fat), 67 mg chol., 1,272 mg sodium, 65 g carb., 3 g fiber, 34 g pro.

▶ pasta salad with orange dressing

MAKE AHEAD UP TO 24 HOURS

PREP: 30 minutes   CHILL: 2 to 24 hours   MAKES: 4 servings

    6 ounces dried multigrain or regular farfalle (bow tie) or penne pasta
    1 15-ounce can black beans, rinsed and drained
1½ cups green sweet pepper cut into thin thin strips
    1 cup chopped cooked chicken (5 ounces)
 ½ cup thin red onion wedges (optional)
    1 8-ounce carton light sour cream
1½ teaspoons finely shredded orange peel
    3 tablespoons orange juice
 ¼ teaspoon salt
 ¼ teaspoon black pepper
    1 to 2 tablespoons milk
1½ cups lightly packed arugula leaves
    3 tablespoons snipped fresh cilantro

1. Cook pasta according to package directions; drain. Rinse with cold water; drain again. Transfer to a large bowl. Add beans, sweet pepper, chicken, and, if desired, red onion; set aside.

2. For dressing, in a small bowl combine sour cream, orange peel, orange juice, salt, and black pepper.

3. Pour dressing over pasta salad; toss gently to coat. Cover and chill for 2 to 24 hours.

4. Before serving, stir enough of the milk into pasta salad to reach desired consistency. Stir in arugula and cilantro.

Per serving: *390 cal., 10 g fat (5 g sat. fat), 51 mg chol., 624 mg sodium, 57 g carb., 9 g fiber, 23 g pro.*

▶ thai chicken noodle salad

MAKE AHEAD UP TO 24 HOURS

PREP: 20 minutes   CHILL: up to 24 hours   STAND: 5 minutes   MAKES: 6 servings

- 1 2¼- to 2½-pound purchased roasted chicken
- 4 cups water
- 2 3-ounce packages ramen noodles
- ¾ cup reduced-fat creamy peanut butter
- ¾ cup unsweetened light coconut milk
- ¼ cup snipped fresh cilantro
- ¼ cup lime juice
- ¼ teaspoon cayenne pepper
- 1 small seedless cucumber, halved lengthwise and cut into ¼-inch pieces
- 6 green onions, thinly sliced
- ¼ cup chopped cashews

1. Remove and discard skin and bones from chicken. Cut chicken into strips. In a medium saucepan bring the water to boiling. Break up each package of ramen noodles (reserve packets for another use). Add noodles to boiling water; remove from heat. Cover and let stand for 5 minutes; drain. Rinse with cold water; drain again.

2. Meanwhile, in a large bowl whisk together peanut butter, coconut milk, cilantro, lime juice, and cayenne pepper until smooth. Stir in chicken, cucumber, and green onions. Add noodles; toss to combine. Cover and chill up 24 hours. Before serving, stir in cashews.

Per serving: 551 cal., 28 g fat (8 g sat. fat), 113 mg chol., 728 mg sodium, 36 g carb., 4 g fiber, 40 g pro.

Purchase and refrigerate the rotisserie chicken a day ahead of when you plan to make the salad. It's easier to skin the chicken and cut the meat into strips when it's cool.

▶ turkey meatballs in pesto pasta pie

MAKE AHEAD UP TO 24 HOURS

PREP: 30 minutes   BAKE: 50 minutes at 350°F   CHILL: up to 24 hours   MAKES: 6 servings

- 1 egg
- ¾ cup soft bread crumbs (1 slice bread)
- ⅓ cup finely chopped onion
- 3 tablespoons grated Parmesan cheese
- 3 tablespoons finely chopped drained, oil-packed tomatoes
- 1 teaspoon dried Italian seasoning, crushed
- ¼ teaspoon garlic salt
- ⅛ teaspoon black pepper
- 1 pound uncooked ground turkey

- 5 ounces dried spaghetti, preferably whole grain spaghetti
- 6 tablespoons purchased basil pesto
- 1 egg, lightly beaten
  Nonstick cooking spray
- 1 cup ricotta cheese
- 1 cup mushroom pasta sauce
- ½ cup sliced pitted Kalamata olives
- 2 tablespoons water
- ½ cup shredded pizza cheese (2 ounces)
  Snipped fresh basil (optional)

1. Preheat oven to 350°F. Line a 15×10×1-inch baking pan with foil; set aside. For the meatballs, in a large bowl combine the egg, bread crumbs, onion, Parmesan, tomatoes, Italian seasoning, garlic salt, and pepper. Add turkey and mix well. Shape into 1-inch meatballs. Place meatballs on prepared pan. Bake about 20 minutes or until no longer pink.

2. Meanwhile, cook spaghetti according to package directions; drain. Stir in 4 tablespoons of the pesto and the egg; set aside.

3. Coat a 9-inch pie plate with cooking spray. Press spaghetti mixture onto bottom and up sides of prepared pie plate, forming a crust. In a small bowl combine ricotta and the remaining 2 tablespoons pesto; spread on and up the sides of the pasta crust. (To serve today, continue as directed in Steps 5 and 6.)

4. To serve later, cover pasta crust with plastic wrap. Chill up to 24 hours. Place cooled meatballs in a resealable plastic bag. Chill for 24 hours.

5. Preheat oven to 350°F. For filling, in a medium saucepan stir together meatballs, pasta sauce, olives, and the water. Bring to boiling, stirring occasionally; reduce heat. Simmer, covered, about 5 minutes or just until meatballs are heated through, stirring twice. Uncover pasta crust. Spoon filling into pasta crust. Cover pie loosely with foil.

6. Bake for 25 minutes. Sprinkle with pizza cheese. Bake, uncovered, about 5 minutes more or until heated through. If desired, sprinkle with snipped fresh basil.

Per serving: *455 cal., 25 g fat (9 g sat. fat), 153 mg chol., 770 mg sodium, 29 g carb., 4 g fiber, 29 g pro.*

Because meatballs freeze, store, and reheat well, they're ideal for make-ahead batch cooking.

▶ turkey breast stuffed with sausage, fennel, and figs

MAKE AHEAD UP TO 12 HOURS

PREP: 20 minutes   CHILL: up to 12 hours   ROAST: 1 hour 15 minutes at 325°F
STAND: 10 minutes   MAKES: 8 servings

    1 2- to 3-pound boneless turkey breast with skin
  ½ teaspoon salt
  ½ teaspoon black pepper
    8 ounces sweet Italian sausage (casings removed, if present)
  ½ cup thinly sliced green onions (4)
  ⅓ cup snipped dried figs
  ¾ teaspoon fennel seeds
  ¼ teaspoon salt
  ¼ teaspoon black pepper
    1 tablespoon olive oil

1. Place turkey, skin side down, between two pieces of plastic wrap. Using the flat side of a meat mallet, pound lightly from the center to the edges into a square of even thickness. Remove plastic wrap. Sprinkle turkey evenly with the ½ teaspoon salt and the ½ teaspoon pepper.

2. For stuffing, in a medium skillet cook sausage until browned, using a wooden spoon to break up meat as it cooks. Drain off fat. In a medium bowl combine sausage, green onions, figs, and fennel seeds.

3. Spoon stuffing onto turkey. Roll up turkey and stuffing into a spiral. Tie at 2-inch intervals with 100-percent-cotton kitchen string. Sprinkle with the ¼ teaspoon salt and the ¼ teaspoon pepper. (To serve today, continue as directed in Steps 5 and 6.)

4. To serve later, wrap stuffed turkey breast in plastic wrap. Chill up to 12 hours.

5. Preheat oven to 325°F. Remove plastic wrap form chilled turkey roll. Place turkey in a shallow roasting pan. Rub skin with the oil. Roast for 1¼ to 1¾ hours or until turkey is no longer pink (170°F) and an instant-read thermometer inserted into center of the stuffing registers 165°F.

6. Transfer turkey to a cutting board. Cover with foil; let stand for 10 minutes. Remove and discard string before slicing.

Per serving: 287 cal., 17 g fat (5 g sat. fat), 87 mg chol., 472 mg sodium, 5 g carb., 1 g fiber, 27 g pro.

If you can't find boneless turkey breast with skin on, purchase a 4- to 5-pound bone-in turkey breast and remove the bone (or ask a butcher to remove it for you).

▶ ginger-orange-glazed turkey breasts

MAKE AHEAD UP TO 24 HOURS

PREP: 25 minutes   MARINATE: 12 to 24 hours   ROAST: 45 minutes at 350°F   STAND: 5 minutes
MAKES: 8 servings

2 1½-pound skinless boneless turkey breasts
2 cloves garlic, cut into 12 slivers total
1 to 2 small fresh red chile peppers, cut into 12 pieces (see tip, page 29)
¾ cup orange juice
¼ cup olive oil
1 cup orange marmalade
½ cup finely chopped green onions (4)
1 tablespoon grated fresh ginger
1 clove garlic, minced
1 tablespoon orange liqueur or orange juice
1 teaspoon kosher salt
1 teaspoon black pepper
Sliced green onion, chopped chile peppers, and/or orange peel slivers (optional)

1. Using a sharp paring knife, cut 12 slits into the top of each turkey breast. Alternating garlic and chile pepper, tuck a garlic sliver or chile pepper piece into slits. Place turkey breasts side by side in a shallow glass baking dish.

2. In a small bowl combine the ¼ cup of the orange juice and the olive oil; pour over turkey. Cover; marinate in the refrigerator for 12 to 24 hours, turning occasionally.

3. For glaze, in a small saucepan combine marmalade, green onions, the remaining orange juice, the ginger, and the minced garlic. Bring to boiling; reduce heat. Simmer, uncovered, for 5 minutes. Remove from heat; stir in orange liqueur.

4. Preheat oven to 350°F. Remove turkey breasts from marinade; discard marinade. Arrange turkey breasts on a rack in a large roasting pan. Spoon some of the glaze over turkey breasts. (Do not let the spoon touch the uncooked turkey.) Sprinkle with salt and black pepper.

5. Roast for 45 to 50 minutes or until an instant-read thermometer inserted into the thickest part of each breast registers 160°F, spooning some of the remaining glaze over breasts every 15 minutes of roasting. (Do not let the spoon touch the uncooked turkey.) Let stand for 5 minutes before slicing. If desired, garnish with additional sliced green onion, chopped chile peppers, and/or orange peel slivers.

Per serving: *369 cal., 8 g fat (1 g sat. fat), 105 mg chol., 349 mg sodium, 31 g carb., 1 g fiber, 42 g pro.*

If desired, make the glaze and pour it into an airtight container. Chill up to 3 days. Reheat glaze in a small saucepan over low heat before using.

▶ niçoise salad sandwiches

MAKE AHEAD UP TO 4 HOURS

PREP: 20 minutes   CHILL: up to 4 hours   MAKES: 4 servings

- 12 thin slices whole wheat bread, toasted
- 4 butterhead (Boston or bibb) lettuce leaves
- ½ cup very thin fresh green beans, trimmed
- 2 4.5-ounce pouches lemon-pepper marinated chunk light tuna
- 1 medium tomato, thinly sliced
- ½ of a medium red onion, thinly sliced
- 2 hard-cooked eggs, sliced (optional)
- 8 niçoise or kalamata olives
- 1 recipe Fresh Parsley Gremolata Vinaigrette

1. Layer four of the toasted bread slices with lettuce, green beans, and tuna. Layer another four bread slices with tomato, red onion, egg slices (if desired), and olives. Drizzle the eight layered bread slices with Fresh Parsley Gremolata Vinaigrette.

2. Place the tomato-layered bread slices on the tuna-layered bread slices to make four stacks. Top stacks with the remaining four bread slices.

3. Cut each sandwich in half. Wrap each sandwich tightly in plastic wrap. Chill for up to 4 hours before serving.

FRESH PARSLEY GREMOLATA VINAIGRETTE: In a screw-top jar combine ¼ cup vinegar, ¼ cup oil, 2 tablespoons snipped fresh Italian (flat-leaf) parsley, 2 cloves minced garlic, ½ teaspoon finely shredded lemon peel, ¼ teaspoon salt, and ¼ teaspoon cracked pepper. Cover and shake well.

Per serving: 367 cal., 18 g fat (3 g sat. fat), 28 mg chol., 652 mg sodium, 26 g carb., 5 g fiber, 25 g pro.

If you can't find marinated tuna, squeeze the juice from a lemon wedge over drained regular tuna.

▶ salmon satay with cucumber-feta salad

MAKE AHEAD UP TO 1 HOUR

PREP: 30 minutes   MARINATE: 1 hour   GRILL: 6 to 9 minutes   MAKES: 6 servings

1½ pounds fresh or frozen skinless salmon fillet
½ cup bottled white balsamic vinaigrette dressing
3 lemons
1 large seedless cucumber, diced
8 ounces feta cheese, cut into ¼-inch cubes
½ cup chopped red onion (1 medium)
⅓ cup coarsely chopped pitted Kalamata olives
¼ cup olive oil
1 tablespoon snipped fresh mint
1 tablespoon snipped fresh parsley
1 tablespoon snipped fresh dillweed
½ teaspoon salt
¼ teaspoon freshly black pepper
Fresh dillweed sprigs (optional)

1. Thaw salmon, if frozen. Rinse salmon; pat dry with paper towels. Cut salmon into twelve ½-inch-wide strips. In a medium bowl stir together salmon strips and salad dressing. Cover bowl with plastic wrap; marinate salmon in the refrigerator for 1 hour (do not marinate any longer). Thinly slice two of the lemons, cutting six slices from each lemon (12 slices total). Juice the remaining lemon to get 3 tablespoons lemon juice; set slices and juice aside.

2. For cucumber salad, in a large bowl combine diced cucumber, cubed feta cheese, chopped red onion, and olives. Add the lemon juice, olive oil, mint, parsley, 1 tablespoon snipped dillweed, salt, and pepper; stir gently to combine. Cover and chill until ready to serve.

3. Remove salmon strips from marinade, reserving marinade. Thread two salmon strips, accordion-style, onto each of six 12-inch skewers, alternating salmon strips with folded lemon slices.

4. For a gas or charcoal grill, place kabobs on a grill rack directly over medium heat. Cover and grill for 6 to 9 minutes or until fish flakes easily when tested with a fork, turning and brushing once with reserved marinade. Discard any remaining marinade. Serve with cucumber salad. If desired, sprinkle with dillweed sprigs.

Per serving: 490 cal., 36 g fat (11 g sat. fat), 96 mg chol., 844 mg sodium, 16 g carb., 3 g fiber, 30 g pro.

To prevent wood or bamboo skewers from charring or catching fire during grilling, soak them in water for at least 30 minutes before using them. A rectangular baking dish half-filled with water works well for soaking.

▶ farro and pine nut tabbouleh

MAKE AHEAD UP TO 12 HOURS

PREP: 25 minutes   COOK: 30 minutes   CHILL: 2 to 12 hours   MAKES: 4 servings

- 1 cup farro, rinsed and drained, or cooked barley or coarse ground bulgur
- 1 tablespoon pine nuts
- 1 cup coarsely chopped tomato
- ½ of a medium cucumber, halved lengthwise, seeded, and sliced
- ⅓ cup snipped fresh parsley
- ⅓ cup snipped fresh cilantro
- ⅓ cup snipped fresh mint
- ¼ cup chopped red onion
- 2 tablespoons olive oil
- 1 teaspoon finely shredded lemon peel
- 2 tablespoons lemon juice
- 1 clove garlic, minced
- ½ teaspoon salt
- ⅛ teaspoon black pepper
  Thinly sliced or crumbled feta cheese (optional)
  Lemon wedges (optional)

1. In a large saucepan bring a large amount of lightly salted water to boiling. Stir in farro; reduce heat. Simmer, uncovered, about 30 minutes or until tender, stirring occasionally. Drain and cool.

2. Meanwhile, heat a small dry skillet over medium-low heat. Add pine nuts; cook for 2 to 3 minutes or until toasted, shaking skillet frequently to ensure even browning. (Pine nuts can burn quickly, so watch them closely.) Remove from skillet; cool.

3. In a large bowl combine farro, pine nuts, tomato, cucumber, parsley, cilantro, mint, and red onion. For dressing, in a small bowl whisk together oil, lemon peel, lemon juice, garlic, salt, and pepper. Pour dressing over tabbouleh; stir gently to combine. Cover and chill for 2 to 12 hours.

4. If desired, sprinkle each serving with feta cheese. Serve with lemon wedges.

Per serving: 272 cal., 9 g fat (1 g sat. fat), 0 mg chol., 329 mg sodium, 41 g carb., 5 g fiber, 9 g pro.

Although cheese adds flavor and protein to salads, they don't hold well over time. When you make a salad more than 4 hours ahead of serving, wait to add the cheese just before you serve it.

▶ greek spinach-pasta salad with feta and beans

MAKE AHEAD UP TO 2 HOURS

PREP: 25 minutes   STAND: up to 2 hours   MAKES: 6 servings

- 1 5- to 6-ounce package fresh baby spinach
- 1 15-ounce can Great Northern beans, rinsed and drained
- 1 cup crumbled feta cheese (4 ounces)
- ¼ cup dried tomatoes (not oil-packed), snipped
- ¼ cup chopped green onions (2)
- 2 cloves garlic, minced
- 1 teaspoon finely shredded lemon peel
- 2 tablespoons lemon juice
- 2 tablespoons extra virgin olive oil
- 1 tablespoon snipped fresh oregano
- 1 tablespoon snipped fresh lemon thyme or thyme
- ½ teaspoon kosher salt or sea salt
- ½ teaspoon freshly black pepper
- 12 ounces dried cavatappi or farfalle pasta
    Shaved Parmesan or Pecorino Romano cheese

1. In a large serving bowl combine spinach, beans, feta cheese, tomatoes, green onions, garlic, lemon peel, lemon juice, oil, oregano, thyme, salt, and pepper. Cover; let stand at room temperature for up to 2 hours, stirring occasionally.

2. Meanwhile, cook pasta according to package directions. Drain, reserving ¼ cup of the cooking water. Toss cooked pasta and pasta water with spinach salad mixture. Serve warm or at room temperature. Top with shaved Parmesan cheese.

Per serving: *408 cal., 10 g fat (4 g sat. fat), 19 mg chol., 487 mg sodium, 62 g carb., 6 g fiber, 17 g pro.*

▶ mexican-style vegetable lasagna

MAKE AHEAD UP TO 24 HOURS

PREP: 35 minutes   CHILL: 2 to 24 hours   STAND: 40 minutes   BAKE: 30 minutes at 375°F
MAKES: 6 servings

½ **cup chopped onion (1 medium)**
2 **tablespoons olive oil**
6 **cloves garlic, minced**
5 **cups sliced fresh mushrooms**
1¼ **cups sliced yellow summer squash (1 medium)**
¾ **cup chopped red sweet pepper (1 medium)**
½ **cup frozen whole kernel corn**
1 **6-ounce package fresh baby spinach (about 5 cups)**
3 **eggs**
2 **cups cream-style cottage cheese**
1½ **cups crumbled Cojita cheese or shredded mozzarella cheese (6 ounces)**
½ **cup fresh cilantro leaves**
10 **6-inch corn tortillas**
1¾ **cups salsa**

1. Lightly grease a 2-quart rectangular or square baking dish; set aside. In an extra-large skillet cook onion in hot oil over medium heat about 5 minutes or until tender, stirring occasionally. Add garlic; cook and stir for 30 seconds. Add mushrooms, squash, sweet pepper, and corn. Cook and stir for 5 to 7 minutes or until mushrooms are tender and squash is crisp-tender. Stir in spinach. Cook and stir just until spinach starts to wilt. Remove from heat.

2. In a food processor or blender combine eggs, cottage cheese, and 1¼ cups of the Cojita cheese. Cover and process or blend until combined. Add cilantro. Cover and process or blend with on/off pulses until cilantro is chopped.

3. To assemble lasagna, arrange five of the tortillas in the bottom of the prepared baking dish, cutting as necessary to fit. Spread with cheese mixture and vegetable mixture. Top with the remaining five tortillas, cutting as necessary to fit. Spread salsa over tortillas; sprinkle with the remaining ¼ cup Cojita cheese. (To serve today, continue as directed in Step 5.)

4. Cover baking dish with plastic wrap. Chill for 2 to 24 hours. To serve, let stand at room temperature for 30 minutes.

5. Preheat oven to 375°F. Bake, uncovered, for 30 to 40 minutes or until lasagna is set. Let stand for 10 minutes before serving.

Per serving: 441 cal., 22 g fat (9 g sat. fat), 152 mg chol., 1,163 mg sodium, 39 g carb., 7 g fiber, 26 g pro.

To freeze corn and flour tortillas, squeeze out the air from the original packaging, then place in a resealable plastic freezer bag. Freeze up to 8 months. Place tortillas in the refrigerator or on the counter to thaw.

▶ white beans and couscous with fresh tomato sauce

MAKE AHEAD UP TO 24 HOURS

PREP: 25 minutes   CHILL: 8 to 24 hours   MAKES: 4 servings

- 1 recipe Fresh Tomato Sauce
- 1¼ cups boiling or very hot water
- 1 cup whole wheat couscous
- 1 teaspoon olive oil
- ½ teaspoon salt
- ½ teaspoon black pepper
- 1 15-ounce can no-salt-added cannellini beans (white kidney beans), rinsed and drained
- ¼ cup crumbled feta cheese (1 ounce)
- 2 tablespoons pine nuts or chopped walnuts, toasted (see tip, page 52)
- 2 tablespoons snipped fresh basil

1. Prepare Fresh Tomato Sauce; chill as directed.

2. In a large bowl or saucepan combine boiling water, couscous, oil, salt, and pepper. Cover and let stand for 5 minutes. Fluff couscous with a fork. Stir in beans, feta cheese, pine nuts, and basil. Serve salad with Fresh Tomato Sauce.

FRESH TOMATO SAUCE: In a medium bowl combine 1¼ pounds fresh tomatoes (about 4), cored and chopped; ½ cup chopped fresh basil; 2 tablespoons olive oil; 2 cloves garlic, minced; ½ teaspoon salt; and ½ teaspoon black pepper. Cover and chill for 8 to 24 hours.

Per serving: *406 cal., 14 g fat (3 g sat. fat), 8 mg chol., 729 mg sodium, 58 g carb., 12 g fiber, 15 g pro.*

sweets ▶
TO SHARE

You'll receive a warm welcome when you arrive with one of these bake-and-take goodies or freezer treats in hand. This array of cakes, cookies, bars, brownies, and special desserts offers options for any occasion.

recipes

▶▶▶ triple-citrus pound cake

MAKE AHEAD UP TO 1 MONTH

PREP: 20 minutes   BAKE: 40 minutes at 350°F   COOL: 1 hour   FREEZE: up to 1 month
STAND: 12 hours   MAKES: 16 servings

- ½ cup milk
- 2 teaspoons finely shredded lime peel
- 2 teaspoons finely shredded orange peel
- 2 teaspoons finely shredded grapefruit peel
- 1 tablespoon grapefruit juice
- 1½ cups granulated sugar
- 1¼ cups butter, softened
- 3 eggs
- 1 teaspoon vanilla
- 2¼ cups all-purpose flour
- ¾ teaspoon baking powder
- ½ teaspoon baking soda
- ¼ teaspoon salt
- 2 tablespoons butter, melted
- 1 to 2 tablespoons orange juice
- ¾ cup powdered sugar
- Finely shredded lime peel, orange peel, and/or grapefruit peel (optional)

1. Preheat oven to 350°F. Grease and flour a 10-inch fluted tube pan; set aside. In a small bowl combine milk, 2 teaspoons lime peel, 2 teaspoons orange peel, 2 teaspoons grapefruit peel, and grapefruit juice; set aside.

2. In a large mixing bowl beat the granulated sugar and the 1¼ cups butter with an electric mixer on medium speed until light and fluffy. Add eggs, one at a time, beating well after each addition. Stir in vanilla.

3. In a medium bowl stir together flour, baking powder, baking soda, and salt. Alternately add flour mixture and milk mixture to butter mixture, beating on low speed after each addition just until moistened. Pour batter into the prepared tube pan, spreading evenly.

4. Bake for 40 to 45 minutes or until a wooden toothpick inserted near the center of cake comes out clean. Cool in pan on a wire rack for 10 minutes. Remove cake from pan; cool completely on wire rack. (To serve today, continue as directed in Step 6.)

5. Wrap cake in plastic wrap; overwrap tightly with foil. Freeze up to 1 month. To serve, thaw cake in the refrigerator overnight.

6. For icing, in a small bowl combine 2 tablespoons melted butter and 1 tablespoon of the orange juice. Stir in powdered sugar until smooth. If necessary, stir in enough of the remaining 1 tablespoon orange juice, 1 teaspoon at a time, to reach drizzling consistency. Spoon icing over cake. If desired, sprinkle with additional lime peel, orange peel, and/or grapefruit peel.

Per serving: 319 cal., 17 g fat (10 g sat. fat), 82 mg chol., 228 mg sodium, 39 g carb., 1 g fiber, 3 g pro.

▶ peaches and cream bread pudding

MAKE AHEAD UP TO 12 HOURS

PREP: 25 minutes   CHILL: 12 hours   STAND: 15 minutes   BAKE: 40 minutes at 350°F
MAKES: 12 servings

- 12 slices cinnamon swirl bread, halved diagonally
- 1 16-ounce package frozen unsweetened peach slices, thawed, drained, and chopped
- 3 ounces cream cheese, cut into small cubes (see tip, below)
- 8 eggs, lightly beaten
- 2 cups milk
- 1 cup whipping cream
- ½ cup sugar
- 1 teaspoon vanilla
- ½ teaspoon salt
- ½ teaspoon ground cinnamon
- ¼ teaspoon ground nutmeg
- 1 recipe Caramel Sauce
- ½ cup coarsely chopped pecans, toasted (see tip, page 52)

1. In a 3-quart rectangular baking dish, arrange bread half-slices, peaches, and cream cheese. In a large bowl whisk together eggs, milk, whipping cream, sugar, vanilla, salt, cinnamon, and nutmeg. Pour egg mixture evenly over bread mixture. Cover and chill overnight.

2. Preheat oven to 350°F. Let bread pudding stand at room temperature for 15 minutes. Bake, uncovered, for 40 to 50 minutes or until set.

3. Before serving, drizzle bread pudding with some of the Caramel Sauce then sprinkle with pecans. Store any remaining sauce in the refrigerator up to 1 week.

CARAMEL SAUCE: In a medium-size heavy saucepan stir together ½ cup whipping cream, ½ cup butter, ¾ cup packed brown sugar, and 2 tablespoons light-color corn syrup. Bring to boiling over medium-high heat, whisking occasionally; reduce heat to medium. Boil gently for 3 minutes more. Remove from heat. Stir in 1 teaspoon vanilla. Cool for 15 minutes.

Per serving: 473 cal., 29 g fat (15 g sat. fat), 214 mg chol., 431 mg sodium, 45 g carb., 2 g fiber, 9 g pro.

TIP

To make cubing easy, place cream cheese in the freezer for 15 to 30 minutes.

▶ salted caramel pots de crème

MAKE AHEAD UP TO 24 HOURS

PREP: 35 minutes   BAKE: 40 minutes at 325°F   COOL: 30 minutes   CHILL: 4 to 24 hours
MAKES: 8 servings

1¼ cups sugar
¼ cup water
¼ teaspoon salt
1½ cups whipping cream
½ cup whole milk
6 egg yolks
1 teaspoon fleur de sel or other flaked sea salt

1. Preheat oven to 325°F. Place eight 4-ounce pot de crème pots or ramekins or eight 6-ounce custard cups in a large roasting pan; set aside.

2. In a medium saucepan combine sugar, the water, and the ¼ teaspoon salt. Heat and stir over low heat until sugar is dissolved. Using a soft pastry brush dipped in water, brush down any sugar crystals on the sides of the saucepan. Increase heat to medium-high; bring sugar mixture to boiling. Boil, without stirring, for 8 to 10 minutes or until sugar mixture turns amber. Remove from heat.

3. Whisking constantly, in a slow stream carefully add whipping cream and milk (mixture will steam and sugar will harden). Return to heat. Cook and whisk about 2 minutes more or until sugar has redissolved.

4. In a large bowl whisk egg yolks until light and foamy. Slowly whisk whipping cream mixture into beaten egg yolks. Pour mixture through a fine-mesh sieve into a 4-cup glass measure with a pouring spout. Divide mixture among pot de crème pots.

5. Add enough hot water to the roasting pan to halfway up the sides of the dishes. Carefully place pan on the center rack of the oven. Bake about 40 minutes or until edges are set while centers jiggle slightly when shaken. Transfer dishes to wire racks; cool for 30 minutes. Cover with plastic wrap. Chill for at least 4 hours or up to 24 hours.

6. Before serving, sprinkle a little of the fleur de sel on each custard.

Per serving: 327 cal., 21 g fat (12 g sat. fat), 221 mg chol., 302 mg sodium, 34 g carb., 0 g fiber, 3 g pro.

▶ white-chocolate cheesecake with triple-raspberry sauce

MAKE AHEAD UP TO 24 HOURS

PREP: 30 minutes   BAKE: 45 minutes at 350°F   COOL: 2 hours   CHILL: 4 hours
MAKES: 12 servings

 1 cup crushed shortbread cookies (about 4 ounces)
 3 tablespoons finely chopped slivered almonds, toasted
 ¼ cup butter, melted
 2 8-ounce packages cream cheese, softened
 6 ounces white baking chocolate with cocoa butter, melted and cooled
 ⅔ cup sugar
 ⅔ cup sour cream
 1 teaspoon vanilla
 3 eggs
 1 recipe Triple-Raspberry Sauce

1. Preheat oven to 350°F. For crust, in a small bowl stir together crushed cookies and almonds. Stir in melted butter. Press crust mixture onto the bottom of an 8-inch springform pan; set aside.

2. For filling, in a large mixing bowl beat cream cheese and melted white chocolate with an electric mixer on medium to high speed until combined. Beat in sugar, sour cream, and vanilla until fluffy. Beat in eggs on low speed just until combined. Pour filling over crust, spreading evenly. Place springform pan in a shallow baking pan.

3. Bake for 45 to 50 minutes or until center appears nearly set when gently shaken. Cool in pan on a wire rack for 15 minutes. Loosen cheesecake from sides of pan; cool for 30 minutes. Remove sides of pan; cool cheesecake completely on wire rack. (See tip below). Cover and chill for 4 to 24 hours.

4. To serve, cut cheesecake into wedges. Drizzle each serving with Triple-Raspberry Sauce.

TRIPLE-RASPBERRY SAUCE: In a small saucepan melt one 10- to 12-ounce jar seedless raspberry preserves over low heat. Add 1 cup fresh or frozen red raspberries. Heat gently just until sauce simmers. Cool. If desired, stir in 1 to 2 tablespoons raspberry liqueur. Cover and chill until serving time. Makes 1¾ cups.

Per serving: 458 cal., 28 g fat (16 g sat. fat), 116 mg chol., 228 mg sodium, 44 g carb., 1 g fiber, 7 g pro.

▶ grown-up s'mores torte

MAKE AHEAD UP TO 24 HOURS

PREP: 30 minutes   BAKE: 10 minutes at 350°F   FREEZE: 13 to 24 hours   BROIL: 30 seconds
MAKES: 12 servings

- 10 cinnamon graham cracker squares
- ⅔ cup sliced almonds, toasted
- 1 tablespoon sugar
- ¼ cup butter, melted
- 1 quart (4 cups) coffee ice cream, softened
- 1 cup chocolate fudge-flavor ice cream topping
- 1 quart (4 cups) dulce de leche ice cream, softened
- 1 7-ounce jar marshmallow creme
- 2 cups tiny marshmallows
- 1 cup miniature semisweet chocolate pieces

1. Preheat oven to 350°F. For crust, in a food processor combine graham crackers, almonds, and sugar. Cover and process with on/off pulses until crackers are finely crushed. Add melted butter; cover and process with on/off pulses until crumbs are moistened. Press crumb mixture onto the bottom of a 9-inch springform pan. Bake for 10 to 12 minutes or until edges start to brown. Cool on a wire rack.

2. Using the back of a large spoon, spread softened coffee ice cream over cooled crust. Spread fudge topping over coffee ice cream. Freeze about 1 hour or until topping is set.

3. Spread softened dulce de leche ice cream over fudge topping. Cover and freeze for 12 to 24 hours.

4. Position oven rack so top of torte is about 4 inches from the heat source. Preheat broiler. Place springform pan on a baking sheet. Quickly spread marshmallow creme over top of torte. Sprinkle with marshmallows and chocolate pieces.

5. Broil for 30 to 60 seconds or just until marshmallows are golden. Using a warm knife, loosen torte from sides of pan; remove sides of pan. Cut torte into wedges. Serve immediately.

Per serving: 538 cal., 24 g fat (12 g sat. fat), 37 mg chol., 255 mg sodium, 77 g carb., 2 g fiber, 6 g pro.

TIP

To soften ice cream, place it in a chilled bowl; stir with a wooden spoon until it's soft and smooth.

▶▶▶ frozen neopolitans

MAKE AHEAD UP TO 1 MONTH

PREP: 25 minutes   FREEZE: 5 hours to 1 month   STAND: 15 minutes   MAKES: 48 servings

          4 cups chocolate-flavor crisp rice cereal
     1¼ cups chopped toasted almonds
          2 tablespoons butter
          2 cups tiny marshmallows
          1 pint (2 cups) chocolate ice cream
          1 pint (2 cups) vanilla ice cream
          1 pint (2 cups) strawberry ice cream
        ½ cup miniature semisweet chocolate pieces, or ⅓ cup chocolate-flavor syrup or
              strawberry-flavor ice cream topping (optional)

1. Line a 13×9×2-inch baking pan with foil, extending the foil over edges of pan. Butter foil; set pan aside. In a large bowl combine cereal and ¾ cup of the almonds; set aside.

2. In a large saucepan melt butter over low heat. Stir in marshmallows until completely melted. Remove from heat. Add cereal mixture to marshmallow mixture; stir gently to coat. Using a buttered spatula or waxed paper, press mixture firmly into the prepared pan. Freeze for 10 minutes.

3. Let ice creams stand at room temperature for 5 minutes. Spread chocolate ice cream evenly over cereal layer in pan. Freeze about 30 minutes or until firm. Spread vanilla ice cream over chocolate ice cream layer; freeze about 30 minutes or until firm. Spread strawberry ice cream over vanilla ice cream layer. Sprinkle with the remaining ½ cup almonds. If desired, sprinkle with chocolate pieces or drizzle with chocolate syrup or strawberry topping. Cover and freeze for at least 4 hours or up to 1 month.

4. Using the edges of the foil, lift frozen neopolitan out of pan. Cut into 1½-inch squares. Let stand for 10 minutes before serving.

Per serving: *71 cal., 3 g fat (2 g sat. fat), 7 mg chol., 36 mg sodium, 9 g carb., 1 g fiber, 1 g pro.*

▶▶▶ best-ever peanut butter brownies

MAKE AHEAD UP TO 3 MONTHS

PREP: 30 minutes   BAKE: 30 minutes at 350°F
FREEZE: up to 3 months   MAKES: 24 servings

- **4 ounces bittersweet chocolate, coarsely chopped**
- ¼ **cup butter**
- ¼ **cup peanut butter**
- **1 cup packed brown sugar**
- **2 eggs**
- **1 teaspoon vanilla**
- ⅔ **cup all-purpose flour**
- ¼ **teaspoon baking soda**
- ⅛ **teaspoon salt**
- **1 cup chopped chocolate-covered peanut butter cups**
- ½ **cup peanut butter**
- ½ **cup softened butter**
- **1 tablespoon milk**
- **1 teaspoon vanilla**
- **2 cups powdered sugar**
- **Chocolate-covered peanut butter cups, halved (optional)**

1. In a medium saucepan combine bittersweet chocolate, butter, and peanut butter. Stir over low heat until melted. Cool. Preheat oven to 350°F. Line an 8×8×2-inch baking pan with foil, extending the foil over edges of pan. Grease foil; set pan aside.

2. Stir brown sugar into cooled chocolate mixture. Add eggs, one at a time, beating with a wooden spoon after each addition. Stir in vanilla. In a small bowl stir together flour, baking soda, and salt. Add flour mixture to chocolate mixture; stir just until combined. Stir in 1 cup chopped peanut butter cups. Spread batter evenly in the prepared baking pan.

3. Bake for 30 minutes or until set. Cool in pan on a wire rack. Using the edges of the foil, lift brownies out of pan.

4. For the nutty frosting, in a medium bowl combine peanut butter, butter, milk, and vanilla. Beat with an electric mixer on medium speed until combined. Gradually beat in powdered sugar. Spread frosting on brownies. Or cut into 24 bars and pipe nutty frosting in the center of each brownie. If desired, top frosting with peanut butter cup half. Layer brownies between sheets of waxed paper in an airtight container; cover. Store in the refrigerator for up to 3 days or freeze for up to 3 months.

Per serving: *252 cal., 14 g fat (6 g sat. fat), 33 mg chol., 134 mg sodium, 30 g carb., 1 g fiber, 4 g pro.*

TIP

If you forget to leave the butter at room temperature to soften for
30 minutes to 1 hour (depending on the temperature of the room),
microwave it at 50% power in 10- to 15-second intervals until softened.

▶ lemon bars deluxe

MAKE AHEAD UP TO 12 HOURS

PREP: 20 minutes   BAKE: 45 minutes at 350°F   CHILL: 12 hours   MAKES: 18 servings

   2 **cups all-purpose flour**
   ½ **cup powdered sugar**
   1 **cup butter, softened**
   4 **eggs, lightly beaten**
1½ **cups granulated sugar**
   1 **tablespoon finely shredded lemon peel (set aside)**
   ⅓ **cup lemon juice**
   ¼ **cup all-purpose flour**
      Powdered sugar
      Crushed lemon drops (optional)

1. Preheat oven to 350°F. In a large bowl stir together 2 cups flour and ½ cup powdered sugar; add butter. Beat with an electric mixer on low to medium speed just until mixture begins to cling together. Press evenly onto the bottom of an ungreased 13×9×2-inch baking pan or 13½×9½×3-inch disposable foil pan. Bake about 25 minutes or until lightly browned.

2. Meanwhile, for filling, in a medium bowl combine eggs, granulated sugar, and lemon juice. Whisk in ¼ cup flour and the lemon peel. Pour evenly over baked layer.

3. Bake for 20 minutes or until edges begin to brown and center is set. Cool in pan on a wire rack. Cut into bars. Tightly cover bars in pan and chill overnight.

4. Sprinkle bars with additional powdered sugar and, if desired, crushed lemon drops.

Per serving: 184 cal., 9 g fat (5 g sat. fat), 55 mg chol., 66 mg sodium, 25 g carb., 0 g fiber, 3 g pro.

When preparing food to tote to a gathering you can't beat the convenience of aluminum foil pans. Use them to bake in or simply to transport food and other items.

▶▶▶ chocolate and candied orange peel cookies

MAKE AHEAD UP TO 3 MONTHS

PREP: 30 minutes   STAND: 30 minutes   BAKE: 10 minutes at 350°F   THAW: 1 hour
FREEZE: up to 3 months   MAKES: 24 servings

- 7 ounces bittersweet chocolate, chopped
- 5 ounces unsweetened chocolate, chopped
- ½ cup butter
- ⅓ cup all-purpose flour
- ¼ teaspoon baking powder
- ¼ teaspoon salt
- 1 cup granulated sugar
- ¾ cup packed brown sugar
- 4 eggs
- ¼ teaspoon orange extract
- ½ cup candied orange peel, finely chopped

1. In a 2-quart saucepan combine bittersweet chocolate, unsweetened chocolate, and butter. Heat and stir over low heat until smooth. Remove from heat. Let stand at room temperature for 10 minutes. In a small bowl stir together flour, baking powder, and salt; set aside.

2. In a large bowl combine granulated sugar, brown sugar, and eggs. Beat with an electric mixer on medium to high speed for 2 to 3 minutes or until color lightens slightly. Beat in orange extract and melted chocolate mixture until combined. Add flour mixture to chocolate mixture; beat until combined. Stir in orange peel. Cover surface of dough with plastic wrap. Let stand for 20 minutes (dough will thicken as it stands).

3. Preheat oven to 350°F. Line cookie sheets with parchment paper. Drop dough by rounded tablespoons 2 inches apart onto prepared cookie sheets. Bake for 10 to 12 minutes or just until tops are set. Cool on cookie sheets for 1 minute. Transfer to wire racks; cool.

4. To store, layer cookies between sheets of waxed paper in an airtight container; cover. Store at room temperature up to 3 days or freeze up to 3 months. Thaw cookies before serving.

Per serving: 194 cal., 11 g fat (7 g sat. fat), 46 mg chol., 70 mg sodium, 26 g carb., 2 g fiber, 3 g pro.

TIP

Always cool cookies completely before storing, and use airtight storage containers to prevent humidity from affecting cookie texture. Thaw cookies at room temperature in the same container in which they were frozen.

▶▶▶ blueberry-walnut twirls

MAKE AHEAD UP TO 3 MONTHS

PREP: 45 minutes   CHILL: 1 hour + 4 hours to 3 days   BAKE: 10 minutes at 375°F
COOL: 2 minutes   FREEZE: up to 3 months   MAKES: 15 servings

      1 cup butter, softened
  1½ cups sugar
      ½ teaspoon baking powder
      ½ teaspoon salt
      2 eggs
      1 teaspoon vanilla
  3½ cups all-purpose flour
      ½ cup blueberry preserves or jam
  1½ teaspoons cornstarch
      ½ cup very finely chopped toasted walnuts (see tip, page 52)

1. In a large bowl beat butter with an electric mixer on medium to high speed for 30 seconds. Add sugar, baking powder, and salt. Beat until combined, scraping sides of bowl occasionally. Beat in eggs and vanilla until combined. Beat in as much of the flour as you can with the mixer. Using a wooden spoon, stir in any remaining flour. Divide dough in half. Cover and chill dough about 1 hour or until easy to handle.

2. Meanwhile, for filling, in a small saucepan combine blueberry preserves and cornstarch; stir over medium heat until thickened and bubbly. Remove from heat. Stir in walnuts. Cover. Set aside to cool.

3. Roll half the dough between two sheets of waxed paper into an 11-inch square. Spread half the filling on the square, leaving a ½-inch border along the edges. Roll up dough into a spiral. Moisten edges; pinch to seal. Wrap log in waxed paper; twist the ends. Repeat with the remaining dough and the remaining filling. Chill at least 4 hours or up to 3 days. Or freeze for up to 3 months.

4. Preheat oven to 375°F. Line cookie sheets with parchment paper; set aside. Cut chilled or frozen logs into ¼-inch slices. Place slices about 1 inch apart on prepared cookie sheets. Bake for 10 to 12 minutes or just until firm. Cool on cookie sheets for 2 minutes. Transfer to wire racks; cool.

5. To store, layer cooled cookies between sheets of waxed paper in an airtight container; cover. Store at room temperature for up to 3 days or freeze up to 3 months. Thaw cookies before serving.

Per serving: *128 cal., 6 g fat (3 g sat. fat), 22 mg chol., 68 mg sodium, 18 g carb., 0 g fiber, 2 g pro.*

Store different varieties of cookies in separate containers. When combined, soft cookies may make crisp cookies limp. If cookies lose crispness after thawing, bake them at 350°F for 5 minutes.

▶index

▶metric

The charts on this page provide a guide for converting measurements from the U.S. customary system, which is used throughout this book, to the metric system.

product differences

Most of the ingredients called for in the recipes in this book are available in most countries. However, some are known by different names. Here are some common American ingredients and their possible counterparts:

- Sugar (white) is granulated, fine granulated, or castor sugar.
- Powdered sugar is icing sugar.
- All-purpose flour is enriched, bleached or unbleached white household flour. When self-rising flour is used in place of all-purpose flour in a recipe that calls for leavening, omit the leavening agent (baking soda or baking powder) and salt.
- Light-color corn syrup is golden syrup.
- Cornstarch is cornflour.
- Baking soda is bicarbonate of soda.
- Vanilla or vanilla extract is vanilla essence.
- Green, red, or yellow sweet peppers are capsicums or bell peppers.
- Golden raisins are sultanas.

volume and weight

The United States traditionally uses cup measures for liquid and solid ingredients. The chart below shows the approximate imperial and metric equivalents. If you are accustomed to weighing solid ingredients, the following approximate equivalents will be helpful.

- 1 cup butter, castor sugar, or rice = 8 ounces = ½ pound = 250 grams
- 1 cup flour = 4 ounces = ¼ pound = 125 grams
- 1 cup icing sugar = 5 ounces = 150 grams

Canadian and U.S. volume for a cup measure is 8 fluid ounces (237 ml), but the standard metric equivalent is 250 ml.

1 British imperial cup is 10 fluid ounces.

In Australia, 1 tablespoon equals 20 ml, and there are 4 teaspoons in the Australian tablespoon.

Spoon measures are used for smaller amounts of ingredients. Although the size of the tablespoon varies slightly in different countries, for practical purposes and for recipes in this book, a straight substitution is all that's necessary. Measurements made using cups or spoons always should be level unless stated otherwise.

common weight range replacements

Imperial / U.S.	Metric
½ ounce	15 g
1 ounce	25 g or 30 g
4 ounces (¼ pound)	115 g or 125 g
8 ounces (½ pound)	225 g or 250 g
16 ounces (1 pound)	450 g or 500 g
1¼ pounds	625 g
1½ pounds	750 g
2 pounds or 2¼ pounds	1,000 g or 1 Kg

oven temperature equivalents

Fahrenheit Setting	Celsius Setting*	Gas Setting
300°F	150°C	Gas Mark 2 (very low)
325°F	160°C	Gas Mark 3 (low)
350°F	180°C	Gas Mark 4 (moderate)
375°F	190°C	Gas Mark 5 (moderate)
400°F	200°C	Gas Mark 6 (hot)
425°F	220°C	Gas Mark 7 (hot)
450°F	230°C	Gas Mark 8 (very hot)
475°F	240°C	Gas Mark 9 (very hot)
500°F	260°C	Gas Mark 10 (extremely hot)
Broil	Broil	Grill

*Electric and gas ovens may be calibrated using celsius. However, for an electric oven, increase celsius setting 10 to 20 degrees when cooking above 160°C. For convection or forced air ovens (gas or electric), lower the temperature setting 25°F/10°C when cooking at all heat levels.

baking pan sizes

Imperial / U.S.	Metric
9×1½-inch round cake pan	22- or 23×4-cm (1.5 L)
9×1½-inch pie plate	22- or 23×4-cm (1 L)
8×8×2-inch square cake pan	20×5-cm (2 L)
9×9×2-inch square cake pan	22- or 23×4.5-cm (2.5 L)
11×7×1½-inch baking pan	28×17×4-cm (2 L)
2-quart rectangular baking pan	30×19×4.5-cm (3 L)
13×9×2-inch baking pan	34×22×4.5-cm (3.5 L)
15×10×1-inch jelly roll pan	40×25×2-cm
9×5×3-inch loaf pan	23×13×8-cm (2 L)
2-quart casserole	2 L

U.S. / standard metric equivalents

⅛ teaspoon	= 0.5 ml
¼ teaspoon	= 1 ml
½ teaspoon	= 2 ml
1 teaspoon	= 5 ml
1 tablespoon	= 15 ml
2 tablespoons	= 25 ml
¼ cup = 2 fluid ounces	= 50 ml
⅓ cup = 3 fluid ounces	= 75 ml
½ cup = 4 fluid ounces	= 125 ml
⅔ cup = 5 fluid ounces	= 150 ml
¾ cup = 6 fluid ounces	= 175 ml
1 cup = 8 fluid ounces	= 250 ml
2 cups = 1 pint	= 500 ml
1 quart	= 1 litre